PRAISE FOR JAMAICA

"Jamaica Kincaid is an unaffectedly sumptuous, irresistible writer."
—Susan Sontag

"Writers wish for perfect readers, but readers wish even harder for perfect writers and rarely find them . . . Jamaica Kincaid is about as perfect as it's possible to be."
—Carolyn See, *The Washington Post*

"[Jamaica Kincaid] is a consummate balancer of feeling and craft. She takes no short cuts or long cuts, breathes no windy pomposities: she connects herself with being direct . . . So lush, composed, direct, off, sharp, and brilliantly lit are Kincaid's word paintings that the reader's presuppositions are cut in two by her seemingly soft edges."
—Jacqueline Austin, *Voice Literary Supplement*

"Kincaid jumps with grace and ease from the mundane to the enormous, and, fascinated, we believe her."
—David Leavitt, *The Village Voice*

"Of a handful of internationally known West Indian writers, only Kincaid so precisely conveys the dual texture of the smaller islands: the translucent overlay of colonial British culture upon people and places so absolutely alien to England. Gently, she peels back the fragile tissues of religion, vocabulary and manners to expose the vibrant life beneath the imported, imposed customs."   —Elaine Kendall, *Los Angeles Times Book Review*

"Kincaid writes with passion and conviction, and she also writes with a musical sense of language, a poet's understanding of how politics and history, private and public events, overlap and blur."
                    —Michiko Kakutani, *The New York Times Book Review*

JAMAICA KINCAID

AMONG FLOWERS

JAMAICA KINCAID was born in St. John's, Antigua. Her books include *At the Bottom of the River, Annie John, Lucy, The Autobiography of My Mother, My Brother, Mr. Potter,* and *See Now Then,* all published by Farrar, Straus and Giroux. She teaches at Harvard University.

ALSO BY JAMAICA KINCAID

At the Bottom of the River

Annie John

A Small Place

Annie, Gwen, Lilly, Pam and Tulip

Lucy

The Autobiography of My Mother

My Brother

*My Favorite Plant: Writers and Gardeners
on the Plants They Love* (editor)

My Garden (Book):

Talk Stories

Mr. Potter

See Now Then

AMONG FLOWERS

AMONG FLOWERS

A WALK IN THE HIMALAYA

JAMAICA KINCAID

Picador

Farrar, Straus & Giroux

New York

Picador
120 Broadway, New York 10271

Printed in the United States of America
Published in 2005 by the National Geographic Society
First Picador paperback edition, 2020

Photographs by Daniel J. Hinkley

The Library of Congress has cataloged the National Geographic Society
hardcover edition as follows:
Kincaid, Jamaica
    Among flowers : a walk in the Himalaya / Jamaica kincaid.
    p. cm. — (National Geographic directions)
    ISBN: 0-7922-6530-0
    1. Kincaid, Jamaica—Travel—Nepal   2. Nepal—
Description and travel.   I. Title.   II. Series.

PR9275.A583K5632 2005
813'.54—dc22

                                        2004059284

Picador Paperback ISBN: 978-0-374-53810-1

Designed by Melissa Farris

Our books may be purchased in bulk for promotional, educational,
or business use. Please contact your local bookseller or the Macmillan Corporate
and Premium Sales Department at 1-800-221-7945, extension 5442,
or by e-mail at MacmillanSpecialMarkets@macmillan.com.

Picador® is a U.S. registered trademark and is used by
Macmillan Publishing Group, LLC,
under license from Pan Books Limited.

For book club information, please visit facebook.com/picadorbookclub or
e-mail marketing@picadorusa.com.

picadorusa.com • instagram.com/picador
twitter.com/picadorusa • facebook.com/picadorusa

D   10   9   8   7   6   5   4

For Jonathan Galassi

CONTENTS

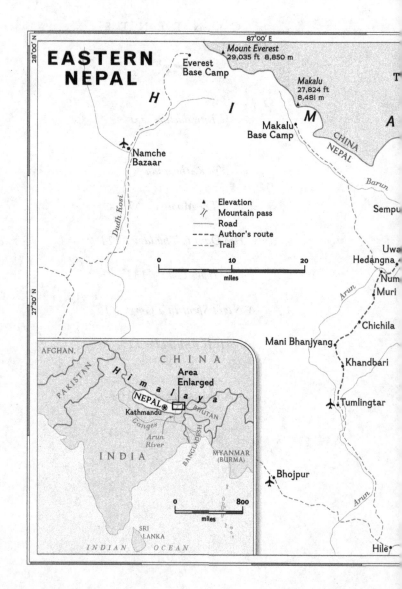

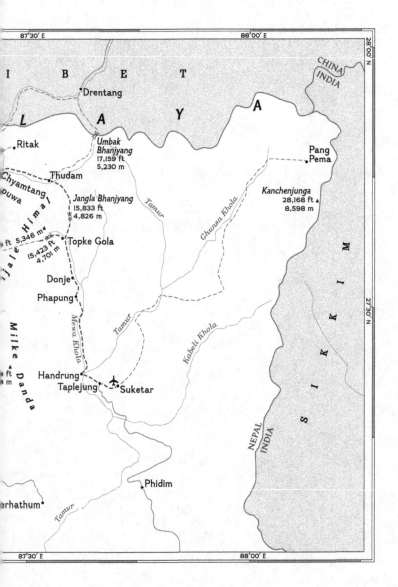

INTRODUCTION

M y obsession with the garden and the events that
take place in it began before I was familiar with
that entity called consciousness. My mother taught me
to read when I was very young and she did this without
telling me that there was something called "The Alphabet"! I became familiar with words as if they were all
wholly themselves, each one a world by itself, intact and
self-contained, and which could be joined to other words
if they wished to or if someone like me wanted them to.
The book she taught me to read from was a biography
of Louis Pasteur, the person she told me was responsible
for her boiling the milk I drank daily, making sure that

the milk would not infect me with something called tuberculosis. I never got tuberculosis but I did get typhoid fever, whooping cough, measles, and a persistent case of hookworms and long worms. I was a "sickly child." Much of the love I remember receiving from my mother came during the time I was sick. I have such a lovely image and memory of her hovering over me with cups of barley water (that was for the measles) and giving me cups of tea made from herbs (bush) she had gone out and gathered and steeped slowly (that was for the whooping cough); for the typhoid fever she took me to the hospital, the Children's Ward, but she visited me twice a day and brought me freshly made juice she had squeezed or grated from fruits or vegetables because she was certain that the hospital would never provide me with the proper nourishment. And so there I was, a sickly child who could read but had no sense of consciousness, had no idea of how to understand and so make sense of the world into which she was born, a world that was always full of a yellow sun, green trees, a blue sea, and black people.

My mother was a gardener but it was as if Vertumnus and Pomona had become one: she was capable of finding something growing in the wild of her native island (Dominica) or the island on which she lived and gave birth to me (Antigua), and if it pleased her when looking at it, or if it was in fruit and the taste of the fruit delighted her, she took a cutting of it (really just breaking off a shoot with her bare hands) or the seed (separating it from its pulpy substance and collecting it in her beautiful pink mouth) and brought it into her own garden and tended to it in a careless, everyday way, as if it were in the wild forest, or as if it were a garden in a regal palace. The Woods: The Garden. For her the wild and the cultivated were equal and yet separate, together and apart. This wasn't as clear to me as I am stating it here, for separation and distinction and interpreting was not at all known to me. I had only just learned to read, and the world outside a book I did not yet know how to reconcile. And so . . .

The only book available to me, a book I was allowed to read all by myself without anyone paying attention to me, was the King James Version of the Bible. No need for me to go here into the troubles of the King James Version of the Bible, only that when I encountered the first book, the book of Genesis, I immediately understood it to be a book for children, and a person, I came to understand much later, exists in the kingdom of children no matter how old they are; even Methuselah, I came to see, was a child. But never mind that, it was the creation story that was so compelling to me for the constant refrain "and saw that it was good"; the God in that book of Genesis made things, and at the end of each day, *saw* that they were good. But, I wondered, for something to be good, would there not be something that was not good, or not as good? That was a problem, though I didn't bother myself with this at the time, mainly because I didn't know how, and also the story had an inexorableness to it: rolling on from one thing to the other without a pause until, by the end of the six days, there were a man and a woman made in God's image, there were fish in the sea and animals creeping on land and birds in the air and plants growing, and God found it all good because here we are.

It was in the week after his creation, the eighth day, that the trouble began: loneliness set in. And so he made a garden, dividing it into four quarters by running water through it (the classic quadrilinear design that is still to this day a standard in garden design) and placing borders, the borders being the eternal good and evil: the Tree of Life, the Tree of Knowledge. One was to be partaken of, the other forbidden. I have since come to see that in the garden itself, throughout human association with it, the Edenic plan works in the same way: the Tree of Life is agriculture and the Tree of Knowledge is horticulture. We cultivate food and only after is there a surplus of it, which produces wealth, so we cultivate the spaces of contemplation, a garden of things not necessary for physical survival. The awareness that comes from that fact alone is what gives the garden its special, powerful place in our lives and imaginations. The Tree of Knowledge holds the unknown and therefore dangerous possibilities; the Tree of Life is eternally necessary and Knowledge is deeply and divinely dependent on it. I can say this now, right now, but it is not a new thought to me—I could see it in my mother's relationship to things she grew, the kind of godlike domination she would display over them. She, I remember, didn't make such a fine distinction between them, she only moved them around when they pleased her, and destroyed them when they fell out of favor.

It is not a surprise to me at all that my affection for the garden and the place where I have encountered some of its most disturbing attributes, its most violent implications and associations, are intertwined with my mother. I did not know myself or the world I inhabited as a child, without her. She is the person who gave me and taught me the Word.

But where is the garden and where am I in it? This memory of growing things, anything, outside not inside, remained in my memory or whatever we call that haunting, trail-like, invisible wisp that is steadily part of our being, and wherever I lived in my young years, in New York City in particular, I planted: marigolds, portulaca, herbs for cooking, petunias, and other things that were familiar to me, all reminding me of my mother, the place I came from. Those first plants were in pots and lived on the roof of a restaurant that only served breakfast and lunch, at 284 Hudson Street, in a dilapidated building whose ownership was not certain, which is the fate of all of us: ownership of ourselves and the ground on which we walk, an ownership of the other beings with whom we share this "and saw that it was good," and of the vegetable kingdom too, is not certain; nevertheless in the garden especially we perform the act of possessing. To name is to possess, to possess is the original violation bequeathed to Adam and his equal companion in creation, Eve, by their very creator, and it is their transgression in disregarding his commands that leads him to cast not only them into the wilderness, the unknown, but also his other possessions that he has designed, not created but designed with much clarity and determination and purpose: the Garden! It is exactly in this way that I enter the world of the garden; for me the garden in the myth of Genesis is a way, perhaps my only way, of understanding and coming to my sole obsession.

The appearance of the garden in our everyday life is so accepted that we know and embrace its presence as sometimes therapeutic, for some people will say that weeding is a form of comfort and settling into misery or happiness. The garden makes managing an excess of feelings—good feelings, bad feelings—rewarding in some way that I can never quite understand. The garden is a heap of disturbance and it might be that my particular history, the history I share with millions of people, begins with the violent removal from an Eden (the regions of Africa from which they came would have been Eden-like, especially encountering the horror, the Fall, which met them in that "New World"). For your home, the place you are from, is always Eden, the place in which even imperfections were perfect and everything after that interrupted Paradise, your Paradise.

Since August 3, 1492, the day Christopher Columbus set sail from Spain and then made a fatal encounter with the indigenous people he met in the "West Indies," the world of the garden changed. That endeavor, to me anyway, is the way the world we now live in began; it affected not just the interior (the way Europeans lived inside and outside changed: Where did the people in a Rembrandt painting get all that stuff they are piling on?), but suddenly they were well-off enough to be interested in more than sustenance, or the Tree of Life (agriculture); they could be interested in cultivating the fruits of the Tree of Knowledge (horticulture).

Suddenly the conquerors could feed themselves and then they could see and want to possess things that were of no use apart from the pleasure they produced to the sight and all the things that leads to. When Cortez saw Montezuma's garden, which was then the lake on which the capital of Mexico now sits, he didn't mention the gardens filled with flowers we now grow with ease in our own gardens (dahlias, zinnias, marigolds).

Let me list some of the ways in which the garden comes into the era of conquest after Columbus: Captain Cook's voyage to regions of the Pacific Ocean that we now know as Australia, New Zealand, New Guinea, Tahiti, and Hawaii, ostensibly to observe the rare event of the transit of Venus, but on this, the first of his four voyages around the world, he took with him the botanist Joseph Banks and also a student of Linnaeus, Daniel Charles Solander, and they took careful notes of everything they saw; it led Banks to decide that the breadfruit, native to islands remote from the West Indies, would make a good food for slaves in the British-owned islands in the West Indies; the slave holders were concerned with the amount of time the enslaved needed to grow food to sustain themselves and the breadfruit grew with ease, in no need of obvious cultivation (to Joseph Banks), and so the Pacific Islands came to the West Indies. It was Joseph Banks who also introduced tea (*Camellia sinensis*) to India.

Where to begin and where to leave off? But there

is no leaving off: there is Lewis and Clark's expedition from the eastern United States to California, and on that adventure, which was authorized by Thomas Jefferson and inspired by Cook's scientific and commercial interest, they listed numerous plants, species that were unknown to John and William Bartram, John being a botanist to George III (for the United States then was still a colony of Britain). William, free of such restraints, wrote a book about his explorations into areas his father had explored before, but without his father's obligation to royal authority. William Bartram's account is said to be an influence on Wordsworth and Coleridge and English Romantic poetry.

There now, look at that: I am talking about the garden, meaning to show how I came to go looking for it in corners of the world far away from where I make one, and I have gotten lost in thickets of words. But it was almost immediately that I started to put seeds in the ground and noticed that sometimes nothing happened, or after paying a large amount of money to make a lawn in the fall and the next spring seeing some red shoots of leaves all over, which led to me cursing the lawn (to myself), that I reached for a book. The first books were about how to make a perennial border or how to get the best from annuals, the usual kind of book for someone who wants to increase the value of their home, but these books were so boring. I found an old magazine meant to help white ladies manage their domestic lives in the 1950s much more interesting (that kind of magazine, along with a copy of *Mrs. Beeton's Book of Household Management*, is worthy of a day spent in bed while the sun is shining its brightest outside). But where did plants, annual and perennial, all to be so pristinely arranged in something called a border and arranged according to color sometimes, the appearance of bloom sometimes, height sometimes, come from? Those books had no answer for me. I then set about finding out what I did not know, and did not even know that I really wanted to know, and so one book led to another (the order I cannot now remember) and before long I had acquired (and read) so many books that it put a strain on my family's budget. Resentment, a not unfamiliar feature of a garden, began to set in. I began to refer to plants by their Latin names and this so irritated my friend and editor at the magazine I then wrote for (Veronica Geng), that she made me promise that I would never learn the Latin names of any plant. I loved her very much and so I promised that I would never do such a thing but did continue to learn the Latin names of plants and never told her. Betrayal, another feature of any garden.

How did plants get their names? I looked to Carolus Linnaeus, who, it turned out, among other things liked to name plants after people whose character of physical feature resembled the plant. Mischief yes, but not too far from the doctrine of signatures, which also made use of plants to cure diseases afflicting the body if the plant resembled the diseased parts of the body. I was thinking about this one day, stooped over in admiration at a colony of *Jeffersonia diphylla*, whose common name is twinleaf. *Jeffersonia diphylla* is a short, woodland herbaceous ephemeral whose six-inch-or-so-wide leaf is divided at the base so that it often looks like a lunar moth, but each leaflet is not identical at the margins and each leaf is not evenly divided: the margins undulate at parts and one leaflet is a little bigger than the other. But isn't Thomas Jefferson, the gardener, the liberty lover, and the slave owner, often described as divided and isn't a plant such as the twinleaf appropriately named for him? The plant was named for him by one of his contemporaries (Benjamin Smith Barton), who perhaps guessed at his true character. It was through this plant that I became interested in Thomas Jefferson and have read, to an alarming degree, much of what he has written, and have opinions about him which I am certain about, including, I will say here, that his book *Notes on the State of Virginia* is a creation story.

And it was Linnaeus that led me to something else. On his way to London for one thing or another, he stopped off in Holland to visit a friend of his, an Anglo-Dutch banker named George Clifford, because Clifford was not well. But Clifford was no ordinary banker, he was a director of the Dutch East India Company. Perhaps because of this position, he had a large greenhouse full of plants from the tropical region of the world. They were unnamed and most likely unknown to Linnaeus, who spent two years in Holland examining these plants and giving them names. He published his findings in a book called *Hortus Cliffortianus*. I paid two hundred dollars for a copy of this book. I can only read it with the help of William Stearn's guide to botanical Latin.

It was only a matter of time before I came to the plant hunters themselves, though its inevitability was not clear to me at all. Look at me: my historical reality, my ancestral memory, of which I am very conscious and which is so deeply embedded in me that I think the whole world understands me before I even open my mouth. A big mistake but a mistake not big enough for me to have learned anything from it. The plant hunters are the descendants of people and ideas that used to hunt me.

The first one I met, in a book of course, was Frank Smythe. I associate my affection for Smythe with Daniel J. Hinkley, though I think Dan thinks more highly of Frank Kingdon Ward, most famous for first finding and introducing the blue poppy (*Meconopsis betonicifolia*), but I always slightly flinch at Kingdon Ward for I have a book of his on which the author photograph on the jacket is of a half-naked Bhutanese man carrying a large suitcase on his back, and written on the suitcase are the words "F. Kingdon Ward," nothing else. However, if you continue to read the book for which this is the introduction, you will find I have described a man carrying my suitcase on his back as I walked up and down some mountains in the foothills of Everest, Makalu, and Kanchenjunga. I have by now reasoned that I didn't need to write my name on my suitcase, for unlike the Bhutanese man and Frank Kingdon Ward, the man carrying my suitcase and I knew each other very well, even though we had never met before.

The special gift Frank Smythe gave to me (apart from the title of this book, from his own exquisite book *The Valley of Flowers*) was his wonderful writing. No one has ever made me think about finding a new primrose or a new flower of any kind so special, like finding a new island in the Caribbean Sea when I thought I was going to meet the great Khan. A new primrose is more special than meeting any conqueror. But he gave me more than that. I noticed when reading him about his plant collecting that he was always going off on little side journeys to climb some snow-covered protuberance not so far away and then days later returning with an account of failure or success at reaching or not reaching the peak, and that by the way he had found some beauty hidden on the banks of a hidden stream and only the sound of water trickling down, or along, revealed to him some new wonder of the vegetable kingdom that would be new to every benighted soul in England. But his other gift to me was the pleasure to be had in going to see a plant that I might love or not, growing somewhere far away. It was in his writing I found that the distance between the garden I was looking at and the garden in the wilderness, the garden cast out of its Eden, created a longing in me, the notion of "to go and to see." Go see!

I end here where I began: reading—learning to read and reading books, the words in books a form of food, a form of life and then knowledge, not a form of knowledge but knowledge itself. But also my mother. I don't know exactly how old I was when she taught me to read, but I can say for certain (she taught my brothers to read in just this way, so it turns out to be nothing particular to me) that by the time I was three and a half years of age, I could read properly and this reading of mine so interfered with her own time to read that she enrolled me in school; but you could only be enrolled in school if you were five years of age and so she told me to remember to answer, if asked, that I was five. My first performance as a writer of fiction or my first performance as a writer? No, not that at all; perhaps this: the first time I was asked who I was. And who am I? In an ideal world, a world in which the Tree of Life and the Tree of Knowledge stand before me, stand before all of us, we ask, Who am I? It turns out we were and still are not given a chance to answer. Among the many of us not given a chance to answer is that woman in the library in St. John's, Antigua, a set of two large rooms that was above the Treasury Department, a building that was steps away from the Customs Office and the wharf where things coming and going through customs lay, and on that wharf worked a stevedore who loaded on ships bags of raw sugar that would be sent to England to be refined into white sugar, a sugar that was so expensive that we, in my family, only had it on Sundays as a special treat; I did not know of the stevedore, lover of this woman who would not allow her children to have white sugar because somewhere in the world of Dr. Pasteur and his cohorts they had come to all sorts of conclusions about diseases and the relationship it had to food (beriberi was a disease my mother tried and apparently succeeded to save me suffering from), that woman, my mother. Her name was Annie Victoria Richardson Drew and she was born in a village in Dominica, British West Indies.

TO KATHMANDU

❧❧

One day, in the year 2000, I was asked to write a book, a small one, about any place in the world I wished and doing something in that place I liked doing. I answered immediately that I would like to go hunting in southwestern China for seeds, which would eventually become flower-bearing shrubs and trees and herbaceous perennials in my garden. Two years before, in 1998, I had done this. I had accompanied the most outstanding American plantsman among his peers, my friend Daniel Hinkley, and some other plantsmen and botanists on a plant-hunting and seed-collecting adventure in Yunnan and Sichuan Provinces. I started out in the city of

Kunming and it was so hot—I wondered if I was just going to have a look at things I could grow in a garden that I made on the island in the Caribbean where I grew up. I wondered if the most thrilling moment I would remember was seeing the tropical version of *Liriodendron tulipifera,* the tulip tree, of William Bartram's travels. But then we went out in the countryside, and up into the mountains, up to fourteen thousand feet in altitude, Dan now reminds me, and I collected seeds of species of primulas, *Iris,* juniper, roses, paeony, *Spiraea, Cotoneaster, Viburnum,* some of which I have now growing in my garden.

I experienced many difficulties in this adventure, but they were of a luxurious kind. I did not like, and could not even bring myself to understand, my hosts' relationship to food: I feel that the place in which it is taken in, eaten, be it the kitchen or the dining room, must be far removed from the place, bathroom or outhouse, in which it comes out again in the form of that thing called excrement. Not once was my life really in danger, not even when I was close by to places where the Yangtze River was in the process of flooding over its banks just at the moment I was driving by its banks in my rather nice, comfortable bus. The greatest difficulty I experienced was that I often could not remember who I was and what I was about in my life when I was not there in southwestern China. I suppose I felt that thing called alienated, but it was so pleasant, so interesting, so dreamily irritating to be so far away from everything I had known.

And so when I was asked to do something I liked doing, anywhere in the world, my experience in southwestern China immediately came to mind. I called up Dan Hinkley and I said to him, Let's go to China again. As a plantsman and botanist, and nurseryman to boot, Dan goes to some faraway place and collects the seeds of plants once or twice a year. The intellectual curiosity of the plantsman and botanist needs it, and the commercial enterprise of the nurseryman needs it also. When I suggested southwestern China to him as a place of adventurous plant-collecting, he said, Oh, why don't we do something really exciting, why don't we go to Nepal on a trek and look for some *Meconopsis*? Why don't we do something really interesting, he said.

In October 1995, Dan had traveled to Nepal on his first seed-collecting expedition there. He had collected in the Milke Danda forest, a forest that is in the Jaljale Himal region. *Milke Danda, Jaljale Himal!* To see those words on a page, flowing from my pen now, is very pleasing to me. In 1998 when I accompanied Dan and some other plants-people to southwestern China, I had no idea that places in the world could provide for me this particular kind of pleasure; that just to say the name of a place, to say softly the name of a place, could cause me to long deeply to be in that place again, or to long just to be nearby again. That first visit he made to Nepal haunted Dan so that he wanted to go there again. It's quite possible that I could hear his longing and the haunting in his voice when he suggested to me that we go looking for seeds in the Himalaya, but I cannot remember it now. And so Nepal it was.

We were all set to go in October 2001. Starting in the spring of that year, I began to run almost every day because Dan had said that the trip would be arduous, that I had no idea how hard it would be, and that I must prepare my body for the taxing physical test to which I would subject it. And so I ran for miles and miles, and then I lifted weights in a way designed to strengthen the muscles in my legs. It was recommended to me that I walk with a backpack full of stones, so that I might make my upper body more strong. I did that. And Dan had said that I needed a new pair of boots and that I should break them in, and so I wore them all the time, in the garden, to the store, or even to a dinner outing. Everything was going along well, until near the end of August: I suddenly remembered that my passport with a visa stamped in it from the Royal Nepalese Consulate General in New York had not come back from my travel agent. I called to tell her that she ought to hurry them up because I applied for my visa in June and here it was August, and still I had not heard if I would be allowed to enter that country in a month. She was very surprised to hear from me, she had not received my passport in June, she had forgotten all about me. In any case where was my passport? We could trace its arrival in her office on Park Avenue, but it never reached her desk. It has been lost, she said; it has been stolen by someone in her office, I thought.

I applied for and within a matter of days received a new passport; I applied for and within a matter of days received a visa to enter and exit Nepal. I had myself inoculated against diseases for which I had not known antidotes existed (rabies) and against diseases I had not known existed (Japanese encephalitis). I felt all ready to go and then there came that new State of Existence into being called "The Events of September 11." How grateful I finally am to the uniquely American capability for reducing many things to an abbreviation, for in writing these words, *The Events of September 11,* I need not offer a proper explanation, a detailed explanation of why I made this journey one year later.

The following spring, the spring of 2002, I resumed my intense training. I trained so hard that near the end of June I was limping, I had done something to my right foot, something that did not show up on an X-ray, only my foot hurt so very much. Then for a short period of time, my son, Harold, who was thirteen at the time, and I determined that he too would make the trip, yes, he would go to Nepal with me, but by the end of August we could see that was not to be. Dan sent me an e-mail asking for our passport numbers and other documents; he wanted to forward them to our guides who would then secure for us our internal travel documents. At that moment Harold said, No, he would not go, as if the whole idea was ludicrous in the first place. Later I would have many opportunities to be glad for his decision. I wrote back to Dan: "So sorry about all this. Harold is not coming but you probably guessed that. Tickets and documents only for me, then. We will share a tent. By the way: Have you heard of the plane crashing and the bus going off the road in the floods, all in Nepal? This happened yesterday. My love to you and Bob."

Just around then, Dan's friends, two botanists who are married to each other and own a very prestigious and famous nursery in Wales, where they live, decided to join us. I have always been so envious of the many seed-collecting trips Dan had made with them to Vietnam, Korea, Japan, and China. Their names are Bleddyn and Sue Wynn-Jones, and the number of times I have heard Dan say that he and Bleddyn and Sue collected something together would fill me with such envy because I really always want to be someplace where seeds are being collected, I want to be in the place where the garden is coming into being. Their presence made me happy and when Dan said, in one of his e-mails, "This is going to be an adventure," it made me forget, for a flash of time, the trouble I was having leaving. This account of a walk I took while gathering seeds of flowering plants in the foothills of the Himalaya can have its origins in my love of the garden, my childhood love of botany and geography, my love of feeling isolated, of imagining myself all alone in the world and everything unfamiliar, or the familiar being strange, my love of being afraid but at the same time not letting my fear stand in the way, my love of things that are far away, but things I have no desire to possess.

I left my home in the mountains of Vermont at dawn one morning at the beginning of October. Nothing was out of place. I made note that the leaves were late in turning, but when I look at a record I keep of things as they occur in the garden I see that I always think the leaves are late turning. It was warm for an early morning in early October, but it is so often warm in early morning in early October. And yet as I drove away from my house, I had the strange sensation that I might be seeing everything in the way I was seeing it for the last time, that when I saw again those things that I was looking at that morning, the mountains (the one I can see from my house, Mount Anthony, in particular), the trees, the houses, the people in their cars, the very road itself, they would not look the same, that the experience I was about to have would haunt many things in my life for a long while afterward, if not forever.

It was only after I returned home a month later that I noticed how quiet and clear are the streams and rivers near where I live; how calmly they meander along as if their paths are old and dull, their origins nearby, not hidden deep within some still unfamiliar place beneath the surface of the earth. Only then I noticed too how smoothed out the sides of the mountains were, not rippling with ridges; how almost uniform in height they seemed, gentle slopes, soft peaks, old and known, with no parts of them unexplored. And the sky above all this? Again, only when I returned home did I notice that the sky above me hardly ever caused me to observe it with real anxiety, being mostly clear and a sad pale blue in the daytime and turning to a grayish black at night. If I made particular note of water, land, and sky when I returned home, it is only because when I was away, walking in the foothills of the Himalaya, that became the world I knew. I knew with certainty. There, I lived outside all that time; and the distinctiveness of it all, the wide and open spaces, were especially so when seen from far away and protected by an overarching and concavelike sky. And this wide-open space was then pursued by the unrelenting encroachment of the mountains, this landscape in the Himalaya.

I left my home on a morning in early October and headed to the airport, which was four hours away. At the time, feeling that it was ridiculously false and then again not so at all, I insisted to myself that everything I saw I was seeing for the last time. This turned out to be true, for when I saw all that I had been familiar with again, everything was changed in my eyes, and yet it did remain the way it had always been, only that I did not see anything the same way again.

I left my home, I went to an airport in New York. I arrived there in the middle of the day. The airport seemed deserted, or spare of human emotion, or just unsettling in a chemically induced way, but I had not ingested a chemical of an unusual kind, as far as I knew. I got on the airplane. All the time my state of mind was influenced by the hard fact that my thirteen-year-old son had not wanted me to go away. That he had said goodbye to me with tears rolling down his cheeks; that he had, days before, asked people he thought could influence me, to tell me outright, my going away to this place, for such a long time, would cause him to suffer.

I love my children, more than I love myself, and yet there I was on an airplane off to Hong Kong and then to Nepal.

On the way to Kathmandu, I spent less than twenty-four hours in Hong Kong; and this small amount of time had the feeling of being a particle of some sediment in a bottle that was being shaken up. Oh, the whirl of it. I was not here or there or anywhere. I was at the airport, again, and the flight was eight hours late. I was sent to a part of the airport where people with destinations different from mine were waiting. A modern airport is not unfamiliar to me. I have been in one of them many times, waiting to go from one place or the other. In a modern airport you will suddenly be confronted with people who are very different from you even though you are all wearing the same sort of clothes, and who have very different ideas from you about how the very world in which you place step after step ought to be arranged. I am used to that. But even so in Hong Kong, in the airport, I felt strange: alone, lonely, excited, happy, afraid, despair, all at the same time. These feelings were exaggerated when I got on the plane, Royal Air Nepal, and was told that the time was not an hour ahead, or an hour behind, but that the time was measured by the quarter hour. It meant that while I could calculate the rest of the world based on that thing called the hour being behind or ahead of me, when I was in Nepal fifteen minutes was lost or gained one way or the other. How confusing is such a thing, how magical is such a thing, how correct is such a thing. Though I only know all of this in retrospect, in sitting at my desk in Vermont and thinking about it, in looking back. We flew to Kathmandu in the dark of night. I childishly asked if it was safe to do so, wondering if we might accidentally crash into a mountain. We landed safely and I gave a man forty American dollars for carrying my suitcase from the baggage area to the taxi. Everyone was astonished by this amount of money, but I was so grateful to be myself, whatever that was, in one place that I would have paid many times that more just to say, "Hi, I am me." I went to bed and slept soundly through the night in a memorable hotel called the Norbu Linka, memorable because it is the only place I have slept in Kathmandu.

That next morning Dan took me to have my photograph taken for my trekking visa, which is a separate one from my visa to enter Nepal, and he also took me to a store to buy an elegant walking stick, a walking cane made of native wood that had the head of a dog carved at the top, just where your hand gripped it. At another store, we bought chocolate bars and tins of candy. Then we went to the best bookstore in the world—that is if you are interested in the world of exploration—the

Pilgrims Book House, and I bought a book, just for the sake of buying a book, about the first attempt to climb Kanchenjunga. Until that moment I did not know there was a mountain called Kanchenjunga. All that time, I was still in between the things I had left behind in Vermont, my thirteen-year-old son not wanting his mother to go so far away from him, the flat-top mountains, the certainty of, just for instance, the plumbing situation (here is the kitchen, here is the bathroom, the two do not know the other exist). Dan had been in Kathmandu for some days before me and he had sent me an e-mail in which he said it was very hot, so bring suitable clothes. Many days before that he had sent me a long list of suitable clothes I would need for our walk in the mountains where we would gather seeds. This particular e-mail made me bristle with anxiety, but anxiety is never any help at all, and so I took note of it and then ignored it. Dan had titled his e-mail "I'll do your bras if you do my underwear," and he'd written:

> Hi Jams: I am at Sea-Tac—no turning back
> now. I have thought through the trip endlessly
> and hope I have bases covered for us. Just a
> reminder of a few things ... Make sure you
> water seal your boots and make sure you bring
> two pairs—I am taking one low-top and one

high-top. The boots will get soaked eventually, but the more you have them water sealed, the better. I like to do them twice beforehand; put them in the sun and let the leather take on the seal, and then do it one more time. I am bringing extra seal with me for us to use during the trip but this needs to be done now.

The socks are important. Buy polypro liners and then polypro hiking socks. The liners will help wick the water away, both from sweat as well as if we start hiking in the morning with wet feet (there is nothing more rude than putting on cold, wet, stiff, hiking boots). I am taking detergent along and we can do some light laundry washing occasionally. (I'll do your bras if you do my underwear.) I am only traveling with three pairs of underwear—in addition to:

—two pairs of polypro long johns, tops and bottoms
—three polypro t-shirts
—two light weight pants, one which converts to shorts
—one pair of hiking shorts
—six pairs of socks and six pairs of sock liners
—one good pair of gloves and five pairs of light-weight glove liners (these are good as they are

comfortable to wear during the chilly days
without having to wear gloves)
—one wool sweater
—one down vest
—rain parka and rain pants
—one long-sleeved soft fleece jacket to wear in
the camp at night
—a warm pair of camp pants—comfy insulated
pants that I will only wear at night. I will
sleep in my long johns.
—Come up with a suit of clothes that you will
only wear at the end of the day after hiking is
over; it is rather nice to change into something that is basically clean, warm, and dry.
—I bought a good insulated sleeping-bag pad.
This is important—do not buy an inflatable
one. This will keep you warmer and more
comfortable than anything else.
—two water bottles—important
—two pairs of sunglasses in case one is broken or
lost—absolutely necessary to have these as we
will be in snow in full sun.

I have brought three courses of Cipro and I
suggest you get your doctor to give you three as
well—I am also going to take Pepto-Bismol

tabs in Kathmandu as sort of a prophylactic—
they say it works. If we get food poisoning, it
will be in Kathmandu—we will be perfectly
fine while on the trail as long as we only drink
boiled water. Damn—I forgot to bring along
iodine tablets for water purification. Would
you please pick up a bottle for us? I might be
able to buy in Kathmandu but not sure.
Generally we don't need them, however, during
the beginning of the trek and again at the end,
it is HOT hiking and at least I go through gal-
lons of drinking water a day.

As I mentioned before, get a prescription
for altitude sickness—they will know which it
is. We are destined to sleep poorly when we get
that high—but at least we will have each other
to talk to during the night. I experience this
really awful oxygen deprivation/panic attack
thing for the first few nights above 10,000 feet.
The drugs really help that.

I have brought plenty of foot dressing, blister
treatment, so you don't have to bother with that.

I still do not have your flight details and
they will need this in order to meet you at the
airport in Kathmandu. I hope we can fly
together home—at least to Bangkok—and go

out for some luxurious feast to celebrate the end of this experience. I arrive in Bangkok on the 3rd and leave for home on the 5th.

You will need money only in Kathmandu and in transit for meals and lodging (easily we can live for $50/day, I think). I cannot recall if our hotel, the Norbu Linka, takes credit cards or not. Kathmandu is fun, and fun for shopping too— We will have such a good time there together.

Sue and Bleddyn in full swing of training for this—taking six-mile mountain hikes every day, it sounds. Sue will not be in great shape for this, but you two will get along quite well. She is a dear and a trouper. Bleddyn is the one that dove off the cliff after Jennifer when she fell in 1995. He will be very good to have along for us both.

This is going to be so fun Jams—an experience that we will never forget and you will tell your grandchildren ... (There are none yet, are there?)

Much love—my best to Harold and Annie. I am sorry that Harold is not coming along but it will happen next time, yes?

Dan

I had faithfully gone to a store nearby that sells just these sort of clothes, clothes for people who are going mountain climbing or hiking, or just generally going to spend time outdoors for the sheer pleasure of it. I bought everything on Dan's list, though not in the quantities he recommended (more underwear, less socks, sock liners, and glove liners).

My hotel was in that area of Kathmandu called the Thamel District. It is a special area, like a little village separate from the rest of the city. It is filled with shops and restaurants and native European people, who look poor, dirty, and bedraggled. But this is a look of luxury really, for these people are travelers, at any minute they can get up and go home. I had read so much about European travelers in Kathmandu, none of it leaving a good impression; seeing these people then in that place did not make me think I ought to change my mind. Of course, I was traveling with Dan, who is of European descent, but Dan had a real purpose for being in Kathmandu: he is a plantsman, and a gardener, and such a person needs plants. There are many plants worthy of being in a garden in Nepal; Kathmandu is the capital of Nepal.

But to think of Kathmandu again: when I suddenly was in the middle of that part of it, the Thamel, I was reminded of feelings I had when I was a child, of going to something called "the fair," something beyond the every day, something that would end when I was not asleep, when I was not in a dream. I did truly feel as if I was in the unreal, the magical, extraordinary. People seemed as if they had no purpose to being themselves, as if the only reason to be there was just to be there. The tiny streets came to an end abruptly, going immediately from the confusion of authentic and imposter to the solidly real, and the real was always poor and deprived and self-contained. Just outside the window of my hotel was an area enclosed by concrete, of perhaps forty feet by forty feet. It had pipes, with water constantly pouring out of them—it was a communal place for doing things that required water. People were bathing, washing their clothes, or filling up utensils with water. Because of my own particular history, every person I saw in this situation seemed familiar to me. But then again, because of my own particular history, every person I saw in the Thamel was familiar also. The person in the restaurant complaining about the lack of some luxury was familiar, the person at the public baths longing for luxuries of every kind was familiar, the person confused and in a quandary was familiar.

On the night of that first day I spent in Kathmandu, we ate dinner at a Thai restaurant. I cannot now remember what I ate. I did notice that my companions, Dan and Sue and Bleddyn, seemed especially kind and gentle toward me. I thought then that it was because I kept looking up for bats; I am very afraid of them. In Roy

Lancaster's book about his travels in Nepal, he mentions the fruit bats in Kathmandu, saying that they look like weathered prunes, and the idea that bats could look like something to eat was unsettling. I had not seen the fruit bats in any tree so far, and so while sitting at dinner, since we were outside, I kept looking out for them. I thought I would see them swooping around in the deep blue-black night air, hoping to realize the sole purpose of their existence: settling into my hair. But I never saw them, not even one. My companions' kind concern toward me was because going back and forth in back of me was a very busy other kind of mammal, a rat. Eventually, I saw it, and I freaked out but only a little. I made a tiny squeal, I shuddered a little bit, but it was as if instinctively things were immediately being put in perspective: what is a lone rat scurrying in a small restaurant in a crowded city next to a small village situated in the foothills of the Himalaya full of Maoist guerrillas with guns?

I awoke the next morning to the sounds of the Himalayan crow crowing outside. It is a beautiful bird, black-feathered like the crows I am used to seeing but with a broadish band of gray around its neck. This band of gray is more like a decorative belt than a necklace, and it makes the crow seem less menacing, more friendly, as if it is not capable of the devious cunning of the crows

I am used to seeing here in North America. And when seen from afar, a large number of them grouped together winging their way toward some unknown-to-me destination, they looked like a thin, worn, ragged piece of darkened cloth adrift.

I went to breakfast and ate something with curry and mango and bananas, doing this with a feeling of getting into the local spirit of things. The king had dismissed Parliament, and I wondered how that would affect our trip, for the king's dismissing Parliament had something to do with the Maoist guerrillas, and I was going into the countryside where the Maoist guerrillas might be, and since they couldn't kill the king would they kill me instead? What was I doing in a world in which king and Maoists were in mortal conflict? The irony of me getting into the local spirit of things was not lost on me, but this feeling of estrangement was soon replaced altogether with a sense of being lost in amazement and wonder and awe. From time to time I lost a sense of who I was, what I thought myself to be, what I knew to be my own true self, but this did not make me panic or become full of fear. I only viewed everything I came upon with complete acceptance, as if I expected there to be no border between myself and what I was seeing before me, no border between myself and my day-to-day existence. My tent, for instance: I loved my tent and would have probably died for it, and am now so glad things never came to that.

After breakfast, I sorted out my luggage, putting away my traveling clothes and shoes and jewelry in a plastic bag, leaving them with the hotel for safekeeping. All four of us had to do this, and this little event suddenly filled us with the excitement of what we were about to do. There was a lot of running up and down the hallway, into each other's rooms, and asking questions about who had what and did they have enough of it. A last-minute run to a bank, for me, and finding it closed; running to another one and finding it also closed, but it had a cash machine. I was told I needed a certain amount of money so that, at the end of our journey, I would be able to tip the porters and Sherpas properly. And then I was with my companions and our Sherpa guide, a man named Sunam, in a little bus heading toward the airport. On our way to the airport we passed by the Royal Palace, where the king and his family live, and I should have been properly interested in that, but I was not at all. Along the palace walls are some enormous trees, junipers, and in them were fruit bats hanging upside down and asleep. I so badly wanted to see them. I craned my neck out the window, looking up as the bus in a swift crawl passed by, but I could not see them. They were there; everyone, even the driver, could see them, but I could not. Dan would say, "There's some, there's some," but my poor eyes, influenced by a combination of the anxiety, wonder, and strange happiness that I was feeling, could not see the fruit bats. We boarded an airplane that made my anxiety dominate all the other feelings. It resembled something my children would play with in the bathtub, rounded and dullishly smoothed, like an old-fashioned view of the way things will look in the old-fashioned future, not pointed and harshly shiny like the future I am used to living in now.

And so we left Kathmandu and flew to Tumlingtar, a village in the Arun River valley. We were not long in the air when the scene changed from crowded city to high green hills. I would have called the hills mountains, but surrounding the hills, in back of the hills, were taller heights covered with snow. These hills ended in sharp, pointed peaks and they were tightly packed one against the other, and covered in what seemed to be an everlasting and inviting green. It was my first view of the geography of the Himalaya. From inside the plane it seemed to me as if we were always about to collide with these sharp green peaks; I especially thought this would be true when I saw one of the pilots reading the day's newspaper, but when I told this to Dan, he said that the other times he flew in this part of the world, the pilots always read the newspaper and it did not seem to affect the flight in a bad way. He then showed me the Arun River, a body of water that I came to count on for many days afterward, as a friendly reference. We landed at Tumlingtar at three o'clock in the afternoon. It was ninety-six degrees Fahrenheit, and I knew without doubt that such a thing—ninety-six degrees Fahrenheit at three o'clock in the afternoon—was a normal occurrence.

The plane had seemed to drop out of the sky. I was worried about it landing, as I had been worried about it getting up into the air and staying there. It didn't so much land as it seemed to be skidding across a field of short green grass. We alighted and I put on my backpack, got my walking stick, and walked out toward our campsite, which I could see was just beyond the area of the airport. The airport itself was occupied by soldiers, evidence of the dreaded Maoists, and they were wearing blue-colored camouflage fatigues. Why blue, and not green (for forest) or brown (for desert), did not remain a mystery for too long. In Nepal, the sky is a part of your consciousness, you look up as much as you look down. As much as I looked down to see where I should place my feet, I looked up to see the sky because so much of what happened up there determined the earth on which I stood. The sky everywhere is on the whole blue; from time to time, it deviates from that; in Nepal it deviated from that more than I was used to, and it often did so with a quickness that brought to my mind a deranged personality, or just ordinary mental instability.

What I was about to do, what I had in mind to do, what I had planned for more than a year to do, was still a mystery to me. I was on the edge of it, though. Here I was in a village in the foothills of the Himalaya. I could still remember the feeling of living in a village in the mountains of Vermont. I could remember that when I spoke, everybody I knew, everybody I was talking to, understood me quite well. I could remember the school building in my village, a nice, very big red brick building that was properly ventilated and properly heated and had all sorts of necessities and comforts, and yet I had found much fault with it and had refused to send my children to school there. I could remember the firehouse just down the hill from where I live and the kind people who volunteer their life to taking care of it and rescuing me if I should need rescuing. I could remember my house with its convenient and fantastic plumbing and water to be had any time I needed it, just by opening the tap in my fantastically equipped kitchen. I could remember my doctor, a man named Henry Lodge, who I often believe exists solely to reassure me that I am not about to drop dead from some imagined catastrophic illness. I could still remember my supermarket, The Price Chopper, overflowing with fruits and vegetables from

Florida, California, or Chile, just so I could choose to buy or not buy, strawberries for instance, in summer, winter, any time I liked.

I walked into our camp, something I would do for many days to come, an hour after our plane landed. That sight of the tents and people milling around would become familiar to me. There were three tents set up, one for Sue and Bleddyn, one for Dan, and one for me. But Dan and I were appalled at spending our nights in separate tents, and so we immediately told Sunam that we wanted to sleep in the same tent and that the tent meant for one of us should become the baggage tent. Perhaps he was used to people like us, perhaps something from his own culture informed him that this was not a bad thing, perhaps he knew that there were more important things in this world than who slept in the same tent with whom; he said okay, that word exactly, "Okay," he said.

I put my backpack inside my tent and while doing that realized that it was an inferno in there. I came out and realized it was an inferno out there. I was wearing some wonderful pedal pusher–type hiking pants— bought at a store in Vermont where all things regarding the outdoors are presented as fashionable—woolen socks, sturdy and altogether well-made boots, a T-shirt made of some microfiber or other. It would have been nice to be wearing less.

I then met my other traveling companions, the people who would make my journey through the Himalaya a pleasure. There was Cook; his real name was so difficult to pronounce, I could not do it then and I cannot do it now. There was his assistant, but we called him "Table," and I remember him now as "Table" because he carried the table and the four chairs on which we sat for breakfast and dinner. Lunch we ate out of our laps. There was another man who assisted in the kitchen department and I could not remember his name either, but we all came to call him "I Love You," because on the second day we were all together as a group, he overheard me saying to my son, Harold, after a long conversation on the satellite telephone, "I love you," and when he saw me afterward, he said in a mocking way, "I love you," and we all, Sue, Bleddyn, Dan, and I, laughed hard at this. He was a very good-looking man in any Himalayan atmosphere and light, and once, many days afterward, when we were very high up and it was very cold, he took a silk scarf he mostly wore around his neck and placed it bonnet-fashion on his head, and then tying it under his chin he looked like Judy Garland, if she had come from somewhere in Asia. But Judy Garland or no, we could never remember his real name, and always he was known as "I Love You." Apart from Sunam, our other personal Sherpas were named Mingma and Thile. There were many other people, all attached to our party, and they were so important to my safety and general well-being but I could never remember their proper names, I could only remember the person who carried my bag, and this from looking at his face when I saw him pick up my bag in the morning. This is not at all a reflection of the relationship between power and powerless, the waiter and the diner, or anything that would resemble it. This was only a reflection of my own anxiety, my own unease, my own sense of ennui, my own personal fragility. I have never been so uncomfortable, so out of my own skin in my entire life, and yet not once did I wish to leave, not once did I regret being there.

We walked into Tumlingtar to see what it was like and also to buy something, anything. We thought, beer would do. Our camp was pitched in an almost already-harvested field of something, a non-vining bean or a legume of some kind. On the other side of the field was another set of trekkers, real trekkers, people who were going off to camp at the base camp area of Makalu, not people like us, who were only going to collect seeds of flowers. One group was from Austria but we decided to call them the Germans, because we didn't like them from the look of them, they were so professional-looking with all kinds of hiking gear, all meant to make the act of hiking easier, I think. But we didn't like them, and

Germans seem to be the one group of people left that can not be liked just because you feel like it. The other group was from Spain. It was to them I turned when I could not make my satellite telephone work. They couldn't make it work either. One night later, when I was especially worried about Harold, I looked hard at the telephone and saw that the antenna was loose and only needed me to snap it in place.

The main road in Tumlingtar was not like a road I was used to: paved with tar and a yellow line down the middle, it was more like a wide, well-worn path. It is a trailhead for going to Mount Everest or Makalu and so people there are quite used to seeing some of the other people in the world. They were used to seeing people who looked like Bleddyn, Sue, and Dan, people of European descent. They were not used to seeing people like me, someone of African descent, but they knew of our existence. I noticed that women in general and old people and children were very friendly and spoke to us with a smile and in a friendly way. The men did not. They looked us up and down and did not speak to us at all, only to each other about us. It was in Tumlingtar that I bought a pair of rubber flip-flops. They were stacked up, in every store we passed, all of them the same. In fact all the stores carried the same things, but I was sure that there were some differences between them that would be obvious to their regular patrons and not at all to me. We walked to the very last building in Tumlingtar and found it to be a restaurant with a patio and proper restaurant tables and chairs. We sat down and ordered beer. It was not ice cold and this was not important. From there we could see up into the hills where people were living, and the houses were surrounded by neatly terraced gardens where mostly food was growing, and we could see cows and chickens, a very familiar domestic kind of situation. It was here we met the sole schoolteacher for all the pupils who went to school in Tumlingtar and the health-care provider for all the people who needed health care in this town. The schoolteacher took us to his school and the four us felt that a good thing to do when we came back to our own overly prosperous lives would be to send money or books to him when we returned home. It was the way we felt then and the way I still feel now as I am writing this. But it only remains a feeling, a strong feeling. I have done nothing to make this something beyond my feelings. I asked the health worker what were the most common diseases to afflict people and he said headaches and fevers and accidents, so I said the word *AIDS,* and he said the word *sometimes.* It was almost dark by the time we returned to our tents. There weren't any electric streetlights or television, or any other distraction from the warm and soft blackness of the night.

We had our dinner in the dining tent, a large blue tent inside which we could stand up, not the small sleeping tent. Inside the tent was a small collapsible table like one used for playing cards and four collapsible metal chairs. The table was covered with a nice blue tablecloth and set with eating utensils and paper napkins. The civility of this stunned me. When I saw the man whose job it was to carry the table and chairs wherever we went, I was appalled that someone had to carry this whole set of civility, especially when so many times it would have been far more comfortable to sit on the ground with our legs tucked under us. And we could not pronounce or even remember this man's name, and that is how we came to call him "Table." He was always among the last to leave camp because he cleaned up after us, and the first to arrive wherever we were going, to make things ready for us.

We went to bed at around nine o'clock that night, the latest we were up. There was still the excitement of the new, there was still lots of chatter and lingering. In any case, we were not tired. Dan and I lay in our tent laughing and chatting for such a long, loud time that the next day Sue and Bleddyn asked us to tell them what was so funny. It was only Dan telling me about a journey he had just made to South Africa with another botanist and how awkward it had been to observe someone who was married, and having an affair, start up yet another affair, and the unexpected arrival of the lover who was not the husband, bearing flowers and chocolates. That night too, I began reading *The Kanchenjunga Adventure,* Frank Smythe's book about an attempt made to climb Kanchenjunga in 1930, a book I had bought at the Pilgrims Book House in Kathmandu. Until that moment I don't think I had ever heard the name Kanchenjunga before. But I was drawn to it as if a spell had been cast over me; first the book and then the mountain, and all the way on my walk, there was nothing I wanted to see more. For my twenty some days I spent walking among the hills of the Himalaya, I lugged this book around; and for many days after I got back, this book was like a child's comforter to me.

To Khandbari: Dan and Bleddyn seem to have gone over the map again and again. Should we go by the way of Jaljale Himal and the Milke Danda, more or less the way they had gone before in 1996, or should they go another way, the first three days of which would be the same as the last three days of that 1996 trip? They went back and forth, finally deciding that yes, the first three days of this trip should repeat the route of the last three days of the 1996 trip. This decision was of great importance to these two nurserymen, for a seed-collecting journey is so difficult. Every square foot of terrain must be carefully pored over so that not a single garden-worthy plant is missed, the poor collector not knowing if he will ever be able to come this way again. A true nurseryman is a gardener, a gardener is a person of all kinds, but in particular a gardener is a person who at least once in the gardening year feels the urge to possess completely at least one plant. This form of possession excludes mere buying or being one of the three people in the world who owns something that is variegated or double flowering when the norm is not. This form of possession comes from seeing something in seed on the knife-sharp edge of a precipice and collecting those seeds, and only after the seeds are in a bag realizing that for a few seconds possibly your life was in question. You can hear this form of possession in the voice of someone who will utter a sentence like this: "I saw some *Codonopsis* growing up there, couldn't tell which one it was but I took seeds anyway." That is no ordinary sentence said in an ordinary voice. The person who says such a sentence is in a complicated state of craving, for they are aware that they haven't invented *Codonopsis,* but having found it in its natural growing area, a place where most people who grow *Codonopsis* as an ornament would shun living, they feel godlike, as if they had invented *Codonopsis,* as if without them no one growing *Codonopsis* as an ornament would do so. Dan and Bleddyn are nurserymen. Sue, of course is a nurseryman too, but she is a different kind of nurseryman. Sue was always quite happy to point out to Bleddyn and Dan a plant in seed as she walked along to our destination.

The nurserymen had decided we would follow the Arun River, spend a day going up the banks of the Barun River starting where it emptied into the Arun, then come back to the Arun leaving it behind when we turned to go toward the fabled village of Thudam.

That first morning, that very first morning after we left Kathmandu, would soon become routine: being awoken at half past five by Table, who brought us a cup of hot tea and a basin of hot water for washing up. I love to be in bed and hate getting out of it quickly, so I lingered then, and always lingered every morning after that. Dan was always first out of our tent, immediately packing up his sleeping bag and mattress, making ready his day pack; and then performing a set of calisthenics— sits-ups and push-ups, all adding up to five hundred repetitions. That first morning when I saw him stretching and twisting, it looked like such a good idea I decided to join him the next day. In the days to come my enthusiasm waxed, waned, and disappeared altogether in that order, and that quickly.

It was already hot at six o'clock in the morning. We had a delicious breakfast of omelet, oatmeal porridge with hot milk, and pancakes. The morning was beautiful, the sky was blue, not the impersonal blue of the sky that I was used to, but as if it was specially tinted that way; and even though it was a wide open sky, very big, it felt confined, as if it was more like a ceiling than a sky. And this confusing notion—sky or ceiling—only grew more so; for a sky is a part of the earth, it is the thing to which you might be exposed, the unfeeling elements raining down on you come from the sky; a ceiling, on the other hand, is the structure that protects you from the sky.

At exactly half past seven in the morning we left camp. We walked through the town of Tumlingtar, the very way we had been the afternoon before where we had met the schoolteacher and the health-care worker, but I didn't see either of them. I didn't see anyone from the evening before and I left the place with a feeling of theoretical sadness, for it was sad that I might never, would never, see any of these people again, or see this place again, and a final parting is a time to feel sad. And so I walked out of the village, up my first official incline. It wasn't at all a very big one, but since I had never just walked up a hill as an everyday thing, I usually drove up a hill as an everyday occurrence, I felt challenged by it. Also, I was influenced by people's warnings about heights and sudden exertion and Himalayan heat. I walked up the incline and thought how good to get that over with and saw that there was another incline and another incline, but then there was a leveling off, but then there were more inclines and then the heat got hot. The path we were walking on was the size of a narrow road, gouged out of the red clay. We walked up a gradual incline, the sun getting a hot I had never known. Up, up we walked, each plateau the beginning of a new, gradual ascent. By midmorning we had gained some height—I could see that—I could look back and see where we had been. But I was used to going somewhere and arriving quickly, and so had to clamp down on feeling impatient. And, there was nothing to collect, certainly nothing I could grow from this climate in the one in which I actually live. I could see *Ricinus,* marigold, and *Datura, Cosmos,* sunflowers growing in people's gardens, and also plots of corn. Below us was the broad, flowing Arun, winding its way down to the Ganges. We passed people who seemed native to India, other people who seemed native to Nepal, and other people who seemed from somewhere in between.

I cannot tell now exactly when in those first few hours of the morning on my journey that my understanding

Nepalese gathering Rhododendron, *their primary fuel source*

JAMAICA KINCAID

of distances collapsed. I walked through the town of Tumlingtar and the way out led to a sharp incline and then to a set of houses surrounded by cultivated plots that seemed to be resting on a plateau, level ground, but the ground was never level for long, and suddenly, or eventually, I was climbing again, going up and up, and the going up seemed sudden, surprisingly new, for I had not expected it. For those first few hours, I was expecting the landscape to conform to the landscape with which I was familiar, gentle incline after gentle incline, culminating in a resolution of a spectacular arrangement of the final resting place of some geographical catastrophe. But this was not so. I walked up toward a ridge, and I thought that when reaching the ridge my whole being would come to something, the something that had made me there in the first place. But this was never to be so. The Himalaya destroys notions of distance and time, I thought then, plant-hunting destroys all sorts of notions, but this I have always known.

The road then, sometimes as wide as a dirt driveway in Vermont, sometimes no bigger than a quarter of that, was red clay unfolding upward; the top of each climb was the bottom of another. By midmorning my senses were addled. It took me many days to realize, to accept really that I was going up; it took me many days to understand how far up *up* was, how there was no real up, how going up was just a way of going there. I began to have a nervous collapse, but fortunately there was no one in my company, botanist, Sherpas, and porters, to whom I could make my predicament matter. Dan had told me of the practice in Nepal of planting two *Ficus* trees together, *Ficus benghalensis* and *Ficus religiosa,* providing shade for the traveler, who from time to time turns out to be people like us. We passed by three such plantings and stopped to drink water, and then at the fourth one we stopped for lunch. As we walked we had been accompanied by a band of children, though not the same ones all the time. As some of them left, others would take their place. When we stopped for lunch, they crowded around and stared at us in silence. They watched us as we ate our lunch. It felt odd but also seemed fair: we were in their country looking at their landscape after all. That day, our first day of stopping to eat lunch, began with cups of hot orangeade, a drink that seemed then extravagant and unnecessary, tasting so hot and sweet, but later we would come to count on and look forward to it. According to the watch I wore on my left hand, a watch that was equipped to do all sorts of things that I could not make sense of, tell direction for one, it was ninety-six degrees and we were in the full heat of the sun all the time we walked. Sue had been walking with her umbrella open, shading herself. When in Kathmandu she had told me about bringing along an umbrella, I had secretly thought it an unnecessary thing to do; now I saw why and I could only look at her with envy.

We continued on our way that afternoon, the scenery remaining the same as the morning, except we came upon a family who lived in a small house that was in the shade of a huge citrus tree, a tree with fruits larger than grapefruits. At about half past one we came into Khandbari, a town that had telephones connected to the world from which I had just come. I called my son, Harold, spoke not to him but to someone who could say to him that I had called him, and went from feeling pleased with myself for that to feeling sad because I had not been able to tell him that I loved him myself. By that time, it was less than a week since I had been away from my home, but I began to wonder what exactly separated me from their memory of me. I was not dead, but might I as well be? Still, might-as-well is different from the certainty.

We passed through Khandbari and almost got into trouble because Dan had left his passport in Kathmandu and Khandbari had a checkpoint. I saw Sunam, our lead Sherpa and guide, speaking to a man in military uniform with an intensity and rapidity I had only seen in movies, and so had thought invented for presentation in a theatrical situation, but it worked in the same way; we were allowed to go on. We reached the place where we would spend the night, a village called Mani Bhanjyang, but the best spots had been taken by the two groups of trekkers who were on our same route. They were going to Makalu Base Camp, and we were on the same route as they for the next two days. Sunam found a place for us to camp down from that in the middle of a field, the only other level piece of earth in the vicinity. We were thirty-seven hundred feet up and even then the sky was beginning to be darker and more curved than I had ever known it to be. That night, I called Harold on my satellite phone and spoke to him directly.

It was that next morning that I began to see the flora of Nepal. We had left our campsite at half past six in the morning and started walking toward what, I did not know yet. It was ninety-six degrees by seven, according to the watch I wore, and we walked up and up for two hours straight. In fact we were just walking through, and also just walking toward, the end of our journey, but I did not know this yet. I still had the idea that we would walk to something and then leave it for something else. But that was never so. We were walking, and every place we walked was something, every place we walked was important, certainly from the point of view of a gardener.

It was just that this gardener lives in Vermont. In any case we were walking, and it was very warm and I kept my eyes closed, in a way, because the climate I was walking in was not the climate in which I make a garden. The climate in which I was walking, the things growing there would count as annuals for me. As a gardener, I have a fixed view of annuals. They really are ornamentals. That is, they are ornaments for the more substantial and, so, really real perennials. In any case, we were walking and I was with Sue. For Dan and Bleddyn had raced ahead as would always be the case, and suddenly I saw these pink flowers everywhere—at my feet when I looked down and somewhat above eye level when I looked up, and then alongside me when I was just going forward. I recognized them from shape and texture, only I had seen them in another color, deep purple. I had seen those same flowers in a nursery in Vermont and in a garden in Maine but only in deep purple. To see them now in pink while remembering them in purple enhanced my feeling of anxiety and alienation, and so when I said to Sue, "What is this?" and she answered me matter-of-factly, "That's *Osbeckia*," I was comforted.

The plant I had seen in the nursery in Vermont and in my friend's garden in Maine had a dark fleshy-colored and coarse-skin stem with deep purple flowers. I had always wanted to plant them in my garden, but they seemed as if they were not really annuals, they seemed too late-blooming and too woody in stem for my climate. On the whole, in my garden (and all the time I was walking around in Nepal I was mostly thinking of my garden) annuals need to be delicate-looking, while at the same time bearing flowers non-stop as if they do not know how to do anything else. Now as I trudged along, not knowing really where I was going, I was thinking of something I had known in passing, a plant seen in a nursery, and in a garden in Maine, trying to latch on to it as if it were one of the certainties in the whole of life. Much later I learned that the deep purple form of *Osbeckia* comes from Sri Lanka, the one before me was native to the place in which I was seeing it.

That day we walked eight miles going gradually uphill. We stopped for lunch in the middle of a village and I asked for a cola soft drink, and received it. That was the last time such a thing happened. It was then that I began to notice this phenomenon. I saw a girl, about the same age my daughter was then, seventeen, combing the hair of someone else with much careful-ness; she was combing through her familiar's thick head of straight hair because it was riddled with lice. This was all done with a loving fierceness, as if something important depended on it. The person combing the hair used a comb that was fine-toothed and carefully went through the hair again and again, making sections and then dividing again the sections into little sections. This engagement between the delouser and head of hair made me think of love and intimacy, for it seemed to me that the way the person removed the lice from the head of hair was an act of love in all its forms. I saw this scene over and over.

That day, for lunch, the vegetable was something I knew by the name of "christophine" and which was familiar to Sunam by another name in Nepali. It is a soft, fleshy, watery fruit originating from somewhere I do not know but is used as a vegetable by people who come from the tropical parts of the world. It is not grown in Antigua, the island in the Caribbean where I am from, but it was grown on the island of Dominica, the island my mother is from. This vegetable was a staple of her diet when she had lived there, and I was remembering the lengths to which she would go to find it and incorporate it in my diet. I hated it then, and so imagine my surprise to find it for lunch in a small village in Nepal. It was the most delicious thing I ever tasted.

From the place we ate our lunch, the center of a little village full of people and many of the things that come with them, I could see ahead of me, my way forward, a landscape of red-colored boulders arranged as

if deliberate and at the same time the result of a geographic catastrophe. I was making this trip with the
garden in mind to begin with; so everything I saw, I
thought, How would this look in the garden? This was
not the last time that I came to realize that the garden
itself was a way of accommodating and making accept-
able, comfortable, familiar, the wild, the strange.
Above us were some large brown rocks and they
seemed firmly placed. So strange, I thought, How
would I get to them? I thought, Once I got to them, I
thought, Life would be settled, I thought. Much to my
surprise, I walked up to them and was in them, and
found a place to take a pee and then walked some more
into a forest of gingers (*Hedychium*) in flower, skullcaps
in flower, *Osbeckia* in flower, *Euphorbia* in flower,
Arisaema in flower—and the botanists, Dan and
Bleddyn, especially were sad. They were not just sad,
they began to sulk, and Dan complained to me about
all that walking (two days) with no seeds to collect and
Bleddyn complained to Sue (his wife) that there were
no seeds to collect. We were only two days out, Sue
said to Bleddyn. I said to Dan, We were still in the
tropics. But they knew that. The day was hot. Sue had
held her umbrella over her head, protecting herself
from all that heat, and I wished again and again that I
had brought one with me.

The forest of gingers was actually a swath of cultivated farmland. People were farming spices, for local consumption, and when I found this out, their guarded and circumspect relationship to me did not seem so inexplicable. While walking through this forest of the gingers I saw *Dicentra scandens, Agapetes serpens,* an epiphytic rhododendron, *Begonia, Strobilanthes* (blue and white), a yellow impatiens that Bleddyn said was not gardenworthy, *Philodendron, Monstera deliciosa, Hydrangea aspera* (subsp. *Robusta,* Bleddyn said to me), *Tricyertis maculata, Arisaema tortuosum, Amorphophallus bulbifera, Osbeckia.* Except for *Dicentra scandens* (the yellow-flowered climbing bleeding heart) and *Begonia*—though not this particular one—none of the plants were familiar to me.

At half past three in the afternoon we reached the village of Chichila. We had started the morning in Mani Bhanjyang at about four thousand feet and had walked up two thousand feet to Chichila. It was still hot but the clouds were coming in from Makalu, or so I was told, because if the clouds had not been coming, I would have been able to see the great Makalu, a mountain that I had never even heard of until I was nearing Chichila and every passerby greeted me with the word "*Nemaste*" and then "*Makalu*." But we were not going to Makalu. We were going to look for flowers, or rather the seeds of flowers. Walking around the the village I saw little gardens in which were cultivated squash, corn, marigolds, and dahlias. We sat on a public bench in the hot sun and drank some beer we had bought. There was no other way for that beer to be had other than someone carrying it from Khandbari on his back. I had not seen, so far, animals put to this use. We had just started to enjoy how nice it was to sit with a beer in the hot sun after a day of walking up when, suddenly, without warning, it turned cold and windy and rain started to fall. It was as if, suddenly, we were in another day altogether, another day in another season. We moved into the shop where we had bought the beer and sat near a fire that seemed to have been burning all along, as if the people there knew that no matter how hot it got outside, eventually a fire would always be needed inside.

Two things happened as I was sitting inside by the fire drinking my beer: A beautiful woman, with naturally glossed, long black hair, saw my own braided-into-cornrow hair and she found it so appealing that she came and sat beside me to touch my hair. She picked up my long plaits and turned them over and over, and using gestures, she asked if I could make her own hair look like mine. I did not know how to tell her that my hairdo, which she liked so much, was made possible by weaving into my own hair the real hair of a woman from a part of the world that was quite like her own. And then when the rain came, Dan had gone to make sure that all our things were protected from getting wet. When he returned, I noticed a big, dull maroon-colored spot on his calf. I thought it was a peculiar bruise, but it was a leech enjoying life on Dan's leg. We all shuddered, Nepalese and visitors alike, with varying intensity, at the sight of it.

The rain continued through dinner. Our dining tent leaked. We sat at our table, set with knife, fork, spoon, and paper napkin, and kept shifting around to avoid the water coming through our tent, eating by candlelight when from outside came the sounds of digging; it was our Sherpas making trenches that would guide the water away from our sleeping tents. It was so kind, so considerate. I had not thought of the possibility of drowning in my sleeping bag while traveling in the Himalaya.

That next morning (it was the eighth of October, a Tuesday, but it had no meaning for me, no usual meaning, it was another day), we were woken up with a cup of tea. After washing, eating breakfast, and packing up, we were off at seven-thirty. It was eighty-nine degrees Fahrenheit as we started out and the sky overhead was that magical blue innocent of clouds, and clear, though over in the distance, a thick milk-white substance—clouds—continued to hide Makalu from my sight. A mile or so on, I would round a bend, and unless I came this way again, I would have missed my chance to see a natural wonder of the world, a wonder I had not known of before. It was then I had a new feeling, a feeling I had never had before. It was something like fear, but I was not actually afraid; it was something like alienation, but I didn't feel apart from the immediate world around me or apart from my friends, Dan and Sue and Bleddyn. I had been away from my home less than a week, I had two children, I could see their faces in my mind's eye, I had come on this journey all because of the love of my garden. The garden, indeed, for here was Dan furiously trying to photograph a bundle of fodder a man was carrying on his back. The fodder turned out to be *Viburnum cylindricum,* a plant he treasures in his garden in Kingston, Washington. It is a beautiful *Viburnum,* with lance-shaped leaves that are deeply veined and white flowers loosely clustered together. It would be too tender for me to grow in Vermont but right for his climate. Dan followed the man for a little while, clicking away with his camera, recording this fact: a garden treasure for him is animal fodder in its native land.

Our porters had been late with our luggage the day before and so when we got to our campsite in Chichila we couldn't change out of hiking clothes right away, and that had caused some irritation and the beginning of our little complaints. That next morning Dan suggested that we pack a change of clothes in our day pack and so not be dependent on the porters for dry clothes when we got into camp. He had remembered from his last trip here that they had a rhythm of their own: it all started out well, but eventually there would be some problem and porters had to be let go and new ones hired in the next village. Now as we walked on toward Num, the town where we would spend the night, a small worry cropped up: our porters seemed not to be as well-disciplined as the other porters with the other groups. They lagged behind and sometimes would disappear completely. We were in open land. The sky could not be more blue. The sun was a hot I had never experienced; it seemed to penetrate into my skin, going in one way and coming out the other. We marched on, sometimes passing the porters, but then they would rush past us carrying our bags, our tents, our chairs and tables, our food, our everything at an incredible speed. When we passed the porters, our hearts sank; when they passed us and rushed on ahead, we thought of the day's end and our nice tents with sleeping bags waiting for us. We came to a little village that appeared to be the Himalayan equivalent of a truck stop. There was a shop, dark inside, and men were coming in and out. There was a lot of shouting and even drunkenness. It interested me greatly to know what was going on. Sunam would not let us linger to see anything or buy anything, but he had not so much control over the porters. We then descended into a forest the floor of which was littered with a chestnutlike fruit, but Dan and Bleddyn couldn't quite agree on what this was, and I could see it was because it had no interest for them. I saw a climbing fern and then I saw my first maple, *Acer campbellii*. It wasn't like the maples I am used to seeing, big-trunked, tall, and with leaves like a geometric illustration. It was slender and modest, and the leaves were only notched near the top, almost imperceptibly so. In the forest, the temperature fell to seventy-eight degrees Fahrenheit, and the cool was welcome. All around us we could hear the gurgle of water coming from somewhere and the ground on which we walked was soft with moisture. Dan was looking for another maple, not the *campbellii*, and he could not find it. He remembered from before that he had found it around where we were but now there was neither the tree nor seeds of it. However, he and Bleddyn found *Paris* and *Roscoea, Tricyrtis, Thalictrum,* and *Lithocarpus,* and something they said was fagaceous, but I had no idea what that could mean. Just outside Chichila they had found some *Rosa brunonii* in fruit, though they were not so very excited about that. We emerged from the forest back into the open sun, and I have to say that I began to flag then. At one o'clock we stopped for lunch in the village Muri. What made Muri a village, other than it said so on the map, I will never know. We ate lunch outside the one-room schoolhouse, a lunch that Cook had made inside the school. We had been walking for five and a half hours. It was eighty-nine degrees Fahrenheit. Many times during our walk we thought we would stop for lunch but we could never find a place that had enough flat space for Cook to make our meals, and water with which to cook our food, and then space for us all to spread out and eat. We ate our lunch, fresh vegetables and tinned fish, and some people—inhabitants from Muri or not, we could not know—watched us do so. Some of the children had hair that had lost its natural pigmentation; it had been black but had become blond, a sign that some essential nutrient was missing from their daily diet.

From our lunch spot, we could see Num in the distance. It was not far away at all. A couple of hours' walk and that was mostly downhill. We started out, in the usually gingerly fashion, and then soon were confidently marching along. We walked on paths, sometimes along places that could only accommodate one person passing at a time, so someone would step aside, squeezing themselves into the brush or into a substantial rock.

On the way to Num, we passed by a nicely built house, it looked like a domicile I was used to; it had a house, a barn, and some other outbuildings. This scene of house, barn, outbuildings, did not look prosperous; it looked more like toil and eking out an existence. It looked industrious. I stopped for a rest outside a building that looked like a place where the cows would be kept, and I enjoyed this scene of familiar domesticity. Not long after, while walking all by myself, Dan and Bleddyn in front of me, Sue behind me, I heard Sue let out a muted, sympathetic scream. From behind me, she could see that my back was covered with blood, my nice blue high-tech synthetic T-shirt was covered with my red bodily fluid. A careful search was made of my clothes and my body but the leech was not found, and this left me with the feeling similar to one I had experienced when I was young and living in New York City and was always afraid of drug addicts breaking into my apartment and stealing my things so that they could then go and buy the drugs they craved. My fear of leeches became way out of proportion to the danger they actually posed. Every step I took was more dangerous than the leech burying itself in my upper back. Dan took a picture of my bloodied back and later when I took off the shirt, I was shocked at how much blood had stained its surface.

We got to Num, camped in the center of town, and sought out some beer. There was none at first, but then someone had some. The lack of readily available alcohol would come to be evidence of the presence of Maoists, but we did not know that then. The beer was warm. Num never, ever had ice. Num had no electricity. The beer was delicious. We found a seamstress and that was a good thing, for in the three days since we left Kathmandu we had shrunk. In fact, if there had not been a seamstress our clothes would be just fine. But I now see that we were aware that this would be our last chance to participate in life, that part of life in which you needed things done for you, luxurious things; your clothes needed tending, and your clothes were beyond necessary. We employed the seamstress to take in our underwear, fasten buttons, tighten pants, mend something or other. She did it well and we were very pleased.

That night there was a thunderstorm unlike any I had ever heard or lived through before. Dan and I were in our tent, tightly snuggled into our sleeping bags. It started to rain and the rain felt like water missiles directed at our tent. I was sure at any moment Dan and I would be drenched with water and part of our sleep routine would be sleeping in rain. But the tent remained upright. It was the thunder that was really frightening and remains so even in memory. The sound of the thunder was above and below us, far away and near at once, but whatever direction it came from, however near or far, it was not like any thunder I had ever experienced in real life or the imagination. There was that clapping and that roaring sound that I associate with thunder, but in this case it seemed to come from deep within the earth and the mountains that surrounded Num, and suggested that there was a more profound earth with mountains that was beyond Num. The warlike attack of rain and thunder continued throughout the night and I slept through it, and I was anxiously awake during it and then I slept through it again. We woke up to the continuing rain and then saw that we were completely locked into a thick mass of clouds. We could not see anything beyond twenty feet. We began to plan the day ahead, sitting around in Num, waiting for the weather to change days later, for the rain and the clouds that shut us in looked as if they would be that way forever. Books to be read were set out, journals to be updated, little bits of gossip to be retrieved from the depths of our brains. At about ten o'clock, the rain stopped falling, the clouds began to lift, dissolving into tiny wisps, and then the sun came out and shone with a brightness that seemed as if it had been just newly made. The whole transformation was in five minutes, from frightening and wet gloom, to hot sun and bright dry. Camp was immediately closed up and we were on our way again. We said goodbye to the campers we had met at the beginning in Tumlingtar, the ones from Spain and Germany and France. They were going off to Base Camp Makalu and would get there in seven days. They went right, we went left, and I had no thought of ever seeing them again.

THE MAOISTS

We left the village of Num at half past ten, the day showing almost no sign of the storm or whatever it was that had gone on during the night. We exited the village by going through someone's backyard. They waved at us, calling out the usual Nepalese greeting, *"Nemaste,"* the equivalent of "Good day," Sunam had told me. It was a simple enough greeting, but I couldn't pronounce it properly. I never succeeded in getting myself to say it just the way I had heard it. We started going down, and this as usual meant that sometime before the day was over we would be going up. After three days, I knew with fixed certainty that to go up would lead to going down and vice versa. Up was always so hard and I never greeted it with any pleasure. Down became so hard that at the end of our journey, it took me four weeks for my knees to recover. Still, if we were to find anything worth growing in our gardens (this especially applied to me, since I lived in the coldest garden zone) we would have to go up.

I believe I was so glad to be on the path again, walking and not sitting or lying while a terrific storm, a storm, the fierceness of which I was not familiar, raged around me. In any case the going down seemed like not much to me. We had been mostly going up the day before and had gotten up to six thousand feet. Going up had been very hard, so hard that I began to think it a definition of real mountain climbing. It is not. The thing that I had not yet gotten used to was this: behind every rising was another one, higher and then higher it went. The ease with which I was used to going anywhere and everywhere had sunk deep into me. If I wanted to be someplace, I only had to find a way of transporting myself there. The idea that I had to actually get myself from one point to the other, through my own effort, was hard to take in then and hard to take in even now, months later, as I write this. But what had I imagined when I set out to do this? I had thought I would walk of course, I just did not understand the kind of walking that was required of me. And so it was that day, our fourth day out, I felt that my legs were adjusting to this walk, this path, that cut through huge slippery rocks and fallen tree trunks. I walked carefully, I had to, a couple of times; and I fell flat on my bottom because I had made a misjudgment in my steps.

And then suddenly again, there was that dramatic, magical change that I was fast getting used to. We had started out, just after the rain, and it was still chilly, so much so, that we bundled up in sweaters. Suddenly it was hot. We had gone from a moist, cold, dark forest into open woodland. Suddenly it was so hot that Dan wished for a secluded spot, where there was a stream that flowed into a pool so that he could take a bath. He did not find the two together. As we walked along in that whole forest, far away from everything in the world, secluded spot and stream that flowed into a pool never did meet up. Perhaps to make up for not finding such a thing, we walked into a world of butterflies. At first, there were only bright yellow ones, dancing in the blue clear air just above our heads and in front of our faces, and there were many of them, as if someone or something nearby did nothing but produce such wonders. But then many other different-colored ones came by. And they came in combinations of colors that are always so startling when you find them in nature, and only in

Author crossing one of the precarious bridges spanning the Arun River

nature are such combinations of colors, maroon and green, red and gold, red with black, blue and gray, aqua blue and black, that never seem garish. I had a camera with me but I had no interest in photographing them. I couldn't anyway, they were never still. This was such a pleasant antidote to the leech of the day before. I never did run into such a sight again, a swarm of so many different butterflies, but the leech was a constant worry.

Eventually, we could see the Arun River in the distance. We could also see the bridge over which we would cross it. That first bridge was a pleasant dream compared to some of the bridges I had to cross later, but the Arun at that point was wide and probably deep right there, and the bridge was narrow and long and I had never crossed such a bridge before. It was just before we crossed the bridge that I saw some Nepali script and a drawing of a star (as in red star) in bright red ink on the concrete foundation of the bridge. Maoists, I thought, at last here they are, this is a sign of them. They had forever been on my mind; I had weighed their presence and activities in Nepal before I came. Before I came, Dan had told me they were not killing foreigners and instead of saying back to him they are killing people, so we mustn't go, I was only too glad to be a foreigner and so become exempt from their wrath. Still they were killing people, and I have noticed that when someone starts killing people, though at first they draw a line at the kind of people they will kill, eventually that line gets erased as they start killing some other people. I can't really take the word of people who will kill their countrymen but not me. I only believed Dan because I wanted to, in truth I didn't believe Dan at all. I was afraid that if I ran into the Maoists they would kill me. Still, the thought of the garden and to see growing in it things that I had seen in their natural habitat, to see the surface of the earth stilled, far away from where I am from, perhaps I would be lucky and see only the writings of the Maoists, perhaps I would never, ever see them at all.

I crossed the Arun River on that bridge. It was exactly half past twelve and we were at an altitude of 2,044 feet. Everyone was very encouraging. They had all done it before. Sunam and Mingma and Thile did not laugh at me; the porters did not laugh at me. Sunam waited for me at the other end and told me how brave I had been to do it. He was very kind to me and was always helping me to put the best face on everything I did awkwardly. Early on he had shown me our route on the map, and I must have looked strange for he said, with much forced cheeriness, that it would be very beautiful, as if he knew to someone like me the word was a sedative. Once, when I had, after a great deal of huffing and puffing, got to the top of a ridge, only to see yet another ridge and then beyond that a huge mountain, I asked him the name of the mountain I saw ahead of me. He said, "That is not a mountain, that is a hill and it has no name." Exactly what he said. But of course, there are no hills in Nepal, there are no meadows, there are no valleys, there are only things that might be called hills and meadows and valleys, all of them little interruptions, little distractions in a landscape that is all mountain. I knew there were no hills but when he said that, I became truly silent. Earlier I had asked him about the red markings on the bridge, I had wondered out loud to him (though I whispered it) if that was a sign of Maoists. He said, no, it was just the Nepalese people expressing their opinions in the recent election. Of course, some of those opinions in the recent elections were those of the Maoists. I knew that but I did not say this to him. And another reason I had to take everything he said with a large grain of salt: Whenever people we met seemed to be talking about us, though me in particular (sometimes it was the color of my skin, sometimes it was my hairstyle), if we asked Sunam what they were saying, he would say he didn't understand their language. He would say that they were speaking in a local language that he didn't understand. The mystery of what Sunam did and did not understand became a source of much amusement. What are they saying? we would ask. I don't understand, Sunam would reply. A joke between Dan and me was: "What are they saying?—[a short pause]—I don't understand," and this would make us laugh until we ached in the last places left in our bodies that were not in pain from our exertions.

At half past one and at an altitude of 3,030 feet and temperature ninety-six degrees Fahrenheit, we stopped and had lunch in a place that was not even on the map. It was on the tiny plateau of a steep climb we had just made. It took us an hour to get there from the crossing of the Arun River and it was less than half a mile. Of course Cook and his assistants were there already when we arrived and they had our hot beverage waiting for us. We had a lunch of potato salad, mushrooms, and boiled melon. A young woman sat on the porch of her house, lovingly combing her own very beautiful, long black hair, trying to make it free of lice. From her exquisite strokes, I could see that she had much practice, which meant that it would never be so. She looked very sad and lost in that way people do when they are doing a good thing but only for their own benefit.

We walked through a neatly arranged village with houses made of wood and painted white but it was too early to stop and, in any case, the village seemed to take up all the flat spaces where we could camp. It was hot, tropical, and I recognized plants from Mexico:

bougainvillea, *Dahlia*, marigold, and poinsettia especially. Every house was surrounded by a food garden,
and though I know that is unusual, a food garden, the
way they grew food, squash vines, for instance, carefully
trellised and then allowed to run onto the roof of a
nearby building, was so beautiful, it became a garden.
And in making this observation, I was reminded again
that the Garden of Eden is our ideal and even our idyll,
the place where food and flowers are one. After that,
food is agriculture and flowers are horticulture all by
themselves. We try to make food beautiful and we try to
make flowers useful, but it seems to me that this can
never be completely so. In this village almost every
building had something written on it in red paint and
the drawing of the sun in much the same way I had seen
on the bridge earlier. I did not ask Sunam where we
were, for I suspected it fell into the category of a place
with no name, a place where he did not understand the
language. We walked on and spent the night on the
school grounds of the next village, a village called
Hedangna. That village had a center concentrated
around a little fountain of water, built not for beauty
but for necessity. From the school yard where we
camped, we were surrounded by the most stunning view
of a massive side of a cliff from which poured white, stiff
bands of water. They were waterfalls, but they didn't

seem to fall in the way I was used to. It looked as if they had been set down there on purpose, so constant was the flow. It was so stunningly beautiful in its cruelty. For the people who looked at it, myself included at that moment, could die from want of it. It is very hard to get water for use in this place where there was so much of it. Water could be seen everywhere, but difficult to harness for human uses. After a few days, we looked more like the people who lived in this place than as if we did not. We looked as if we longed to bathe and I smelled that way too. As if to remind us of how the day had begun, just before the sun vanished, not set, vanished, a rainbow suddenly arced out of the clouds that were keeping the tops of the mountains ahead of us in a shroud. For all of that, we calculated that we had walked three miles that day, we were only three miles away from Num, and yet it was another world altogether. As if I was looking, in a manner of speaking, at a set of pictures, of the same event but from different angles and seen at different times of the day. Num was only three miles away. I could even see it across the deep valley from which I had come, but the distance seemed imagined even though I could actually see it.

That night, we were surrounded by more children and adults than usual, and Sunam told me not use my satellite telephone. That was how I knew he was worried the Maoists were around. They came to see us, boys and girls in equal number, so it seemed to me; a man carrying a baby, but he could not have been its father, he seemed so young. An old woman came over to me and literally examined me. She picked up my arm and peered into my eyes and touched and poked my skin; then felt my braids and loudly counted them out in her language, a language which Sunam, I am grateful to say now, told me he did not understand. We went to sleep in our tents, Sue and Bleddyn in theirs, Dan and I in ours. Dan read some of a book he said was very bad; I tried to read my Smythe but found I could not concentrate on his adventure, for I was having my own.

That next morning we left our camp at half past seven. It was eighty-three degrees Fahrenheit. We had eaten a breakfast of rice porridge and omelet with onions. How good everything tasted. How good everything looked. The world in which I was living, that is, the world of serious mountains, the highest peaks in the world, over the horizon, if only I would just walk to them, the world of the most beautiful flowers to be grown in my garden, if only I would just walk to where they were growing. I was trying to do so. That morning, I could see that on the top of one of Sunam's "hills with no name" there was snow. The day before, Bleddyn had said to me that I should try to find *Actaea acuminata*

The author's digital camera offers villagers a rare glimpse of their own images.

because someone named Jamie would give me Brownie points. Dan said we were too low for finding this; Bleddyn said, yes, but soon we would be. I, of course, would have no idea what this plant is even if it were my nose itself. Still, I thought I would look; and much to Dan's and Bleddyn's annoyance, would always say, "What is this?" in my most studentlike voice possible. They were not pleased and I noted they were always way ahead, way out of earshot of me. They found an *Amorphophallus* at an altitude of 4,490 feet and it had seed, which they collected. And that was exciting, though mostly to me, for I had never found an *Amorphophallus* before. I had never even thought of this plant before. It looked like a jack-in-the-pulpit except that the spathe stood upright. Bleddyn thought there was sure to be some *Daphne bholua* growing right around where we were. But we could not find any. Then we came upon a village, again not one found on the map, and there in the yard of one of the houses were sheets of paper hung up on a clothesline, presumably to dry them. Dan and Bleddyn were very excited by this, for *Daphne bholua* is the plant often used for making paper. They ran to the man's house to buy some of the sheets of paper and he must have been very surprised by the sudden increase in his business, but he didn't show, at least not so that I could tell. Dan bought twenty-five sheets,

I bought twelve sheets, Bleddyn bought quite a lot because he needed the paper to dry the leaves of specimens he was collecting. After our little shopping spree (and it did feel wonderful to buy something), the burden of which we simply passed on to our porters, there ensued a small disagreement between Dan and Bleddyn over whether the paper was made of *Daphne bholua* or *Edgeworthia gardneri*. This paper, by the way, was not some exotic thing being made for the use of people far away. It was being made for everyday use by the people in the surrounding area. It made me think of a beautiful young woman I had met the day before in the village of Hedangna. She was returning home to her village with a bag of salt on her back. She had gone to Hile, a big town that has bus service to Kathmandu, and purchased a load of salt. It was six days' walk from her village of Ritak, a village way up near the Tibetan border, to Hile and six days back. She carried with her a little pot and some rice and a thin foam-rubber mat. Often we would pass people going in one direction or the other (though, when they were going in our direction, they passed us easily) who carried on their backs a pot and grain of some kind and their foam mattress; sometimes we passed them cooking their food, sometimes we passed people asleep in the path, as if they couldn't go one step further and just lay down where sleep overcame them.

We were walking now in wide, open, rocky meadows. For a while we walked along a dangerous ledge and there were lots of sighs, on my part. I saw a beautiful yellow *Hibiscus* in bloom; it looked somewhat like *Abelmoschus manihot,* but if it was that, it was the most beautiful form of it I have ever seen. It was a bright, glistening yellow and the blooms were huge. I never found any seed on it. Then we were in deep, moist shade, not exactly a forest, but a shady enough place for there to be found *Codonopsis.* We could smell it though it could not be found immediately. Eventually Bleddyn found a plant with some seed. It was ninety-six degrees Fahrenheit when we stopped to eat our delicious lunch of tinned baked beans, luncheon meat, and spinach. We stopped near a stream that was rushing downhill to meet the Arun, and we sat in it in a place where it made a pool, with all our clothes on.

That afternoon we crossed the Arun River four times, and three of the four bridges were quite sound ones. The one that wasn't I dealt with quietly. That afternoon also we saw some white-haired monkeys way above us in trees, and they made the most wonderful sounds to each other. I was so happy to see them; and this suspicious thought crossed my mind, that I was happy to see them because to see them is to claim them. Claiming, after all, was the overriding aim of my journey. Dan showed me a vine with grapelike leaves and stems covered with golden hairs. It was *Clematis buchananiana,* something new to me. That particular plant had no seed, and though we came across it many times, we never found any with seed and this even I regret.

By the time we made our final crossing of the Arun for the day, we were tired. We wanted to stop and make camp but Sunam said not then. We passed through rice paddies, and untended boggy places. We saw much marijuana growing wild, we saw people smoking the marijuana. Finally, at half past four, seventy-nine degrees Fahrenheit, 3,570 feet altitude, we came to the village of Uwa, the place where we would spend the night and a village under complete Maoist control.

The minute we walked into the village we could see them. There were banners hanging from house to house, and on the banners were portraits of a red sun and, I assume, the same sayings we had seen on the bridge. Sunam had actually reached the village an hour before we did. He usually went ahead of us to make sure our things were all set up for our arrival. But when we got to Uwa, one hour later, the porters were standing around with their burdens at their feet and Sunam was nowhere to be seen. He was actually in negotiations with the head Maoist. The head Maoist either couldn't or wouldn't give us permission to spend the night.

There were many consultations. Finally we had to give them four thousand rupees, and at almost six o'clock we were allowed to go and make camp on the school grounds. To get to the school grounds we had to thread carefully through a rice paddy, carefully because we didn't want to ruin the crop and because we didn't want to get our shoes wet. That was done well enough, and we were just about to sink into the deliciousness of the danger we were in, when we realized our shoes were crawling with leeches that were eagerly burrowing into our thick hiking socks, trying to get some of our very expensive first-world blood. I shrieked of course, then took off my shoes and socks, then searched all the parts of my body that I could and asked Sue to search the parts of my body that I could not. She did and I did the same for her.

Things began to look grim. Sunam thought it would be best if he kept my satellite phone. The Maoist had told him that we would not be allowed to pass on through the village. The four thousand rupees were only for spending the night. We began to think of alternate routes. Sunam really began to think of alternate routes. Around that time, Sue and Bleddyn became Welsh and Dan and I became Canadians. Until then, I would never have dreamt of calling myself anything other than American. But the Maoists had told Sunam that

Village children

President Powell had just been to Kathmandu and denounced them as terrorists, and that had made them very angry with President Powell. I had my own reasons to be angry with President Powell too. In any case I had noticed that all of the bridges I walked on to cross from one side of the Arun to the other had a little notice bolted onto the entrance, thanking a donor for the bridge. The countries mentioned were either Canada or Sweden. I had no idea how familiar Maoists were with people from Canada and Sweden. Canada seemed so broad, non-particular, open-minded. I decided, that if asked, I would say I was Canadian. I didn't feel ashamed at all.

Whenever we had stopped to spend the night in a village, no sooner had we arrived then it seemed all the children in the neighborhood had come to stare at us. A few adults would come too, but mostly it would be children and they would stare at us as we cleaned ourselves, ate, went to bathroom (a little tent that we carried with us and was almost always the first tent to be set up wherever we were), even just sitting around reading. In this village no one came to look at us. All the children seemed to have walked up to a ledge that was right above us, and they climbed into the trees and began to make the sounds that some monkeys, who were also above us and in the trees, were making. It was meant to disturb us but it didn't at all. Nothing could be more disturbing than sleeping in a village under the control of people who may or may not let you live.

The village was situated in a rather strange place and there must be a good reason why people settled in just that spot. It was surrounded on all four sides by high steep cliffs. It was more like a dam, a place made for storing things, than a place to live. It had three openings through which people could come and go. But the cliffs were so high that they shrank even the vast Himalayan sky when seen from the village. That night we did the usual leech check. There was no laughter from our tents. We got up the next morning with the usual tea brought to us by Cook's assistant and an unusual amount of anxiety. Would they let us proceed or send us back? They let us go. Sunam gave them some more rupees, how much more, he wouldn't say. He made them give him a receipt to show to the other Maoists, if we should meet them, that he had already paid what could be made to seem like a toll, but Dan said with surprising anger, that it was extortion. Sunam had learned from someone that we should avoid spending the night or even going near the village we had planned on spending the night in because the people who controlled that village were even more committed to Maoism and took even stronger objection to the words President Powell had spoken in Kathmandu.

We headed out of Uwa at half past seven, so very glad to be leaving. No one spoke to us, not even to say the usual *Nemaste!* What a great hurry we were in. And we started up again, going up away from the Arun. It was good to be up but by going up high so early in the day, it meant something bad for Bleddyn. He had wanted to take a short hike up the Barun River and collect some seeds. How disappointed he was to see it, a thin streak of milky white coming down the mountain and ending in the Arun, which was way below us. He cursed the Maoists. We had been walking for six days now and there had been nothing substantial to collect. Nothing for me anyway. I would have done this, even if I had not been interested in the garden. Just to see the earth crumpling itself upward, just to experience the physical world as an unending series of verticals going up and then going down—with everything horizontal, or even diagonal, being only a way of making this essentially vertical world a little simpler—made me quiet. I saw the people and I took them in, but I made no notes on them, no description of their physical being since I could see that they could not do the same to me. I can and will say that I saw people who looked as if they came from the south (that would be India) and people who looked as if they came from the north (that would be Tibet). I saw some people who were Hindus (they were the same people who looked as if they came from the south), and I saw some people who were Buddhists (they were the same people who looked as if they came from the north).

As usual, we were walking along a ledge and a false step in the wrong direction could land any one of the four of us a few hundred feet down, either in the crown of trees or on sheer rock, for sometimes below us was thick forest, or sheer cliffs at other times. We stopped for lunch after one o'clock. The Arun was in full view and so was the Barun running into it. Even from so far above we could hear the roar of their waters. We stopped for lunch and it was memorable to me because that was the last time we had bread. For dessert, we had toast with marmalade and tea. It was the best toast and marmalade I had ever had, and when eating it I thought, This is all I'll eat for the rest of the time I am here. But when I requested it that night for dinner, I was told that the last of the bread had been eaten at lunch. It dawned on me then that requests were out, and I stopped asking for anything with the expectation that I would receive what I asked for. On again we marched after lunch, feeling a lot better because we could see our village in the distance and also because the collecting was becoming exciting, at least for any gardener who lives in at least two zones warmer than the one in which I make my garden. We were at an altitude of a little under six thousand feet and among the things Dan and Bleddyn collected were some *Hydrangea aspera* subsp. *strigosa, Boehmeria rugulosa, Costus* sp., *Acer* (maple), *Paris polyphylla, Woodwardia* sp., *Anemone vitifolia, Rubus lineatus.*

It was about three o'clock when we arrived in the village, feeling pleased with ourselves for having avoided the Maoists, but something made Sunam change our camping spot. We had met a man who had just lost the tips of three of his fingers on the left hand. Someone must have told him we were coming for he was waiting for us with his hand outstretched, and he was crying. Dan, who always carries a little first-aid kit in his backpack, cleaned the wound and then put some Mercurochrome and a Band-Aid on the man's fingers. We had a little debate over whether to give him any of our Tylenol to relieve him of pain right away since we could not part with enough that might give him some comfort for many days. This ended with Sunam telling us that the village would not be where we would spend the night. We would have to march on a little further up above the village. Whatever he learned about our presence in the village, he never told us. We just were told that we would be camping a little higher up. We then took a road out of the village, going around it, not through it, and seeing some beautiful houses made of clay, painted white with some kind of stencil decoration around the windows and doors. I had seen something similar two nights ago when we stayed in the village of Hedangna, but there the stencil was done in the color brown while here it was done in blue. Bleddyn came across a pink *Convolvulus,* whose fragrance we could smell long before we saw it. But the *Convolvulus* had no seeds and, after the botonists lamented that fact, we just walked on and hoped to find it somewhere else with seed. We saw it twice again but always it was in flower, never having any seed.

Our way now, having left the village, was a steep walk up a landscape that had not so long ago collapsed. We had to climb up and then cross over a recently ravaged hillside (in any other place, it would be a mountainside), that had perhaps not too long ago been the result of a landslide. The evidence of landslides was everywhere, as if proving what goes up must come down is necessary. We, and by this I mean Sue, Bleddyn, Dan, and me, expressed irritation at this with varying intensity (Dan and Bleddyn minor, Sue almost minor, me loudly) and then marched on. Two men, dragging long thick trunks of bamboo attached to porters' straps wrapped around their foreheads, passed us as they were going the other way. They seemed to take our presence for granted, as if they knew about us before they saw us, or as if our presence was typical, or as if we did not matter at all. We marched on; by this juncture we were marching—the leisureliness of walking was not possible once we came in contact with the Maoists. When we got to the top, as usual, it was not at the place of destination. What had seemed to us as the top of the mountain was only the place where the avalanche began. The mountain continued up and it was as if the face of the mountain had decided to fall down starting in its middle. We had to go up some more because, for one thing, Cook, who was always ahead of us—he could walk so fast—could not find any water coming out of the mountain. And also we needed to find some level ground on which to cast our tents, forming our little community of the needy, dependent, plant collectors and the Nepalese people, whose support we could not do without. We kept going up, each turn up above seeming to hold the desirable flatness and water too, for how could that not be so when everywhere we looked we could see a milky white and stiffly vertical flowing line of a waterfall. But Cook went flying up and then went flying down to Sunam, and there were consultations. On our way up, past the place where the avalanche began, we met a herdsman, though before that we had met his cows. At first we made way for the cows because we thought we were in the cows' home and perhaps we should be respectful of them. But the cows remained so cowlike, stubborn and potentially dangerous, if you only considered their horns, and in this case *they* seemed to really consider their horns. The herdsman managed them beautifully, guiding them down and away from us, taking them into the steep bush-covered slopes away from the path they were used to traveling, just to keep us calm. I would not have thought about this incident of the herdsman and his cows again but I saw him the night after this and three nights after this again far away, for me, from all these difficulties.

Porters' loads can exceed one hundred pounds.

Between the cows and their herdsman and Cook not finding water to cook us supper, we grew irritable. From our place way up above the village, and even from that way up above the place where we had eaten our lunch, we were closed in. The sun was setting somewhere; we could see the light growing dimmer, literally like someone turning the wick of a lamp lower. We, and by that I mean me in particular and especially, began to whimper and even complain. For one thing, from our vantage point, so high above, we could see the porters carrying our baggage and the tents and all our other supplies and necessities, resting at the place where we had eaten our lunch. So if Cook should find a place in which to cast camp, and casting camp always depended on him, we—and we were so important we felt then—could not enjoy camp, for the things that made sitting in camp comfortable were half a day's walk away. What had the porters been doing all day? someone said—meaning, What had they been doing when we were exploring the landscape, looking for things that would grow in our garden, things that would give us pleasure, not only in their growing, but also with the satisfaction with which we could see them growing and remember seeing them alive in their place of origin, a mountainside, a small village, a not easily accessible place in the large (still) world? We were then having many emotions, feelings about everything:

The Maoists were right, I felt in particular: life itself was perfectly fair, people had created many injustices; it was the created injustices that led to me being here, dependent on Sherpas, for without this original injustice, I would not be in Nepal and the Sherpas would be doing something not related to me. And then again, the Maoists were wrong, the porters should be fired; they were not being good porters. They should bend to our demands, among which was to make us comfortable when we wanted to be comfortable. We were very used to being comfortable, and in our native societies (Britain, for Bleddyn and Sue; America, for Dan and me) when we were not comfortable, we did our best to rid ourselves of the people who were not making us comfortable. We wished Sunam would fire the porters. But he couldn't even if he wanted to. There were no other porters around.

We were hungry and tired. It really was getting dark. The sun was going away, not setting. We couldn't see it do that, we could only see the light of day growing dimmer. Still, we could see the porters. They were far away. Way below us. The most forward of them were not even near the place where we had come across the fragrant *Convolvulus*. And there was no real place to camp. No doubt I will always remember this evening, for it was the evening where we could not decide where we would stay, among other things. At just about the time some of the porters were traversing the unpleasant landslide, Sunam decided that we would cast our camp at a spot that was the only level site in the area. Cook had found a stream nearby, in any case, and that was always the deciding factor. We were three-quarters of the way up a steep rising of rock covered with some *Taxus* and *Sorbus* and, instantly recognizable to me, barberry and some kind of raspberry *(Rubus).* We made our way through them and found we were in a field that had growing in it mostly wormwood, some kind of *Artemisia.* What a relief. And then someone pointed out a leech and then another and then another, and we soon realized that we would camp, we would spend the night in a field full of leeches.

Immediately as we entered this area we were attacked by them. At first it was just one or two seen on the ground, then leaping onto our legs. Then we realized they were everywhere, like mosquitoes or flies or any insect that was a bother, but most insects that were a bother were familiar to us. The leech was not something with which we were familiar. And why was it so frightening, so strange? It was just a simple invertebrate, after all. But a leech is a different kind of invertebrate. To see it whirl itself around as it gathers momentum to fling itself dervishlike onto its victim is terrifying; to see the way it burrows into clothing as it tries to get next to a person's warm skin so it can first make a gash that cannot be felt, for it administers an anesthetic as it bites, is terrifying; to see a thin, steady stream of blood running down your arm or your companion's arm is terrifying, for the leech also administers in its bite an anticoagulant. Was it because it was silent, making no noise of any kind that made it so reprehensible, so shudder-making? A *leech,* just the mere words would make us jumpy, cross. When Dan had first told me of this journey, he had mentioned leeches as one of the disturbing things to be encountered. He had also mentioned altitude sickness and deprivations of everyday comforts such as showers, bathrooms, people you loved, but I remembered leeches more than I remembered Maoists, even when I got to Kathmandu and saw the evidence of a civil war, soldiers with submachine guns everywhere. I remember Dan saying that there will be leeches but we will have so much fun. That night above the Arun River, on the opposite side of the Barun River, looking into the Barun Valley, I was not concerned with anything but the leeches. And so when we walked into our campsite and I saw these little one-inch bugs whirling around and then leaping into the air and landing on us, my spine literally stiffened and curled. I could feel it do this, stiffen and then curl. I screamed loudly and silently at the same time. And then I did what everybody else was doing, Sherpa, porter, and fellow botanist, I forged ahead, grimaced, laughed, searched for the parasites, found them, and picked them off and killed them with great effort and satisfaction. Even so, the disdain and unhappiness for spending the night in a field of leeches never went away.

The stoves were lit and Cook began to make us food. There was no room for our dining tent so the table and chairs were set out on a tarpaulin. We had tea and biscuits, nothing could stop this—and how grateful we were for this. Night fell suddenly, as if someone, somewhere, decided to turn out the light because it suited them right then. After being hot all day, suddenly we were cold and wanted very much to put on our warm clothes. But the clothes were way down below. Sunam had gone back down to hurry up the porters who were carrying our suitcases. The laxness of the porters made Dan and Bleddyn annoyed not only because they couldn't change into dry clothes but also because they wanted to review their collections of the day, try to do some cleaning of seeds, and make some entrances into the collection diaries. We were sitting on our chairs in the open air and looking out on the Barun Valley at night in the Himalaya. It was beautiful. But the leeches kept coming at us. Finally we set up a sort of Leech Patrol; each person, the four travelers, looking for leeches in four different directions.

Our luggage still had not arrived and there was much discussion regarding what the porters had been up to all day. And there was no *chang,* a fermented beverage made from millet, or any other kind of alcoholic beverage as far as we could tell, in the Maoist area. We—I, really—felt small, as if I were a toy, inside the bottom of a small bowl looking up at the rim and wondering what was beyond. The person who lived in a small village in Vermont was not lost to me, the person who existed before that was not lost to me. I was sitting six thousand feet or so up on a clearing we had made on the side of a foothill in the Himalaya. Only in the Himalaya would such a height be called a foothill. Everywhere else this height is a mountain. But from where we sat, we were at the bottom—for we could see other risings high above us, from every direction a higher horizon. The moon came up, full and bright. And it looked like another moon, a moon I was not familiar with. Its light was so pure somehow, as if it didn't shine everywhere in the world; it seemed a moon that shone only here, above us. It sailed across the way, the skyway, that is, majestically, seemingly willful, on its own, not concerned with having a place in the rest of any natural scheme. It was a clear night. We sat on the tarpaulin, on the chairs around the table in a circle, huddled toward the middle to see more clearly and readily the leeches. We were looking up at the sky, clear and full of stars, the light from the moon outlining the tops of the higher hills, and they *were* hills when placed in context of the true risings beyond which we could not see.

It must have been near nine o'clock when we had our dinner. I should have been hungry but I wasn't. I felt sick, my stomach hurt, I wanted to throw up. I was served but could not eat. Dan said that perhaps it was the altitude. We were up at about six thousand feet. Dan flossed and brushed his teeth. I did not. I don't know what Sue and Bleddyn did. Dan and I went into our tent. He reminded me to check my shoes and socks for leeches, to check myself for leeches, to check the space around my sleeping bag for leeches. All was clear and then we settled in to have our nightly review of the day's events, which mostly resulted in huge cackling and laughter. We had finished our cackling and laughter and were about to go to sleep when there occurred a huge storm of fierce thunder and big rain—the kind of thunder and rain that made me think it was pretending to be so fierce and then I thought it was the end of the world, we would never leave this place, the storm would so change the world that we would be forced to stay in the leech field in our tents forever And it reminded me that this was my first question when confronted with the landscape of the Himalaya: Is this real? It is real enough. We heard Bleddyn calling out to us, Dan and me, that we should check our tent window. Dan and I turned on our flashlights and saw an army of leeches trying to penetrate the window, a square made of mesh netting which served as ventilation on the side of our tent. It was horrifying, not only because we were so far away from everything that was familiar to us. All day as we had marched along, taking a new route to escape the Maoists and their demands, which we felt might include our very lives; we felt endangered, assaulted, scared. In reality it was just about a dozen leeches, but how to explain to a leech that we did not like President Powell? How to tell a Maoist that Powell wasn't even the president? At some point I stopped making a distinction between the Maoists and the leeches, at some point they became indistinguishable to me, but this was only to me. Fortunately I had acquired some DEET, against Dan's advice, that justifiably denounced insecticide, and I always carried it with me. I reached into my day pack, which was at the foot of my sleeping bag, and sprayed it furiously on the leeches trying to get into our tent and they just fell away and I hoped they were dead. I could not sleep. I wanted desperately to pee but when I thought of the leeches leaping up and then burrowing themselves in my pubic hair, I decided to hold it in. But then I couldn't fall asleep and so I went out of our tent, just outside the entrance, and took a long piss. This was a violation of some kind: you cannot take a long piss just outside your tent; you are not to make your traveling companions aware of the actual workings of your body. Not to allow anyone an awareness of the workings of your body is easy to do in our normal lives, where we have access to our own bathrooms, thirty-minute showers of water at a temperature that pleases us, toilets that allow their contents to disappear so completely that to ask where to could be made to seem a case of mental illness. After I had my pee, I took another sleeping pill and went to sleep and did not dream about Maoists, leeches, or anything else. And then I was awakened by a terrifying sound of land falling down from a great height, an avalanche. It sounded quite close by. The morning didn't come soon enough. We got dressed rapidly (I did not brush my teeth), packed up, ate, checked ourselves for leeches, and left. We never wanted to see that place again.

We got going without regret, without looking back, without even wishing for another moon like the one we had seen the night before. It was the most beautiful moon I had ever seen without a doubt, but I would not spend a night in a field full of leeches just to see another one like it. We marched upward the steep climb to the top. Many times the thick growth of maple, oak, *Sorbus,* and yew would thin out and clear up and I felt the top was near, but this clearing was only a pause leading up to more thick forests and darkness and moistness and slippery paths, almost falling down in a way that could be dangerous—and this was not a place to have an accident of any kind. To twist your ankle here wouldn't be good at all; it would cause much misery and inconvenience. Then again, if your heart cracked out here, how much longed-for would a twisted ankle be? We climbed up to nine thousand feet, finally reaching a clearing that was somewhat level. We were at the very top of the ridge of the mountain we had just walked up. Almost as a reward, Dan immediately found a *Cardiocrinum giganteum* that was almost twice as big as the tallest of us, and that was Dan himself. It had lots and lots of seed. How happy he was and Bleddyn too. And after that we seemed to find nothing but *Cardiocrinum giganteum,* they were everywhere. I remained deeply in the experience of the night before: The Moon, The Leeches, The Landslides, The Escape from the Maoists, all of it capitalized. We walked down the forested hillside, plunging into a gulley, going more steeply down it seemed than we had gone up the day before; the sun hot overhead, the sky clear of clouds and blue as if it had never known otherwise. Down we went, toward the Arun again, passing through a thick forest of oak, *Aralia,* and *Berberis.* I kept my eyes peeled to the ground, carefully picking out each step I took, for we were on moist ground. In fact the earth seemed to be only a leaky surface; I could hear water trickling, I could feel my feet slipping on the sticky wet ground. From time to time I fell and cursed myself for doing so. But then we were out in the open sun and the ground was dry and we were walking in nothing but red-fruited *Berberis.* But I couldn't collect any seeds because they are on the list of banned seeds, seeds not to be brought into my country. As usual, our destination seemed farther away the closer we got to it. We could see a village high above the other side of the Arun, and it was the village beyond that was our destination. We stopped for lunch just before crossing a river, that fed into the Arun, at a place called Sampung, and then one hour after lunch crossed the Arun and started climbing up again. That day after the night spent in the field with the leeches, we walked for nine hours and stopped in Chepuwa just a mile or two from our destination, the village of Chyamtang, because it was getting dark. We were so very tired and cross, though not with each other and not with the people who were taking care of us.

When we made camp in the schoolyard in Chepuwa, we were immediately surrounded by children, one of them wearing a T-shirt that had the word *Paris* written on it. His T-shirt referred to the city, not the plant. In fact, though the plant *Paris* was native to the very place he is from, he most likely had never paid attention to it and so had never seen it. In any case, for dinner we had reconstituted food, Chinese food at that. I was not hungry. I went to bed at eight that night and noted that we were at an altitude of seven thousand feet. We had begun the day at six thousand feet altitude, walked up to nine when reaching the top of the hillside on which we had spent the night, walked down to three thousand feet when we crossed the Arun, and now were spending the night at seven thousand feet altitude. If I was suffering from the dreaded altitude sickness, I did not know it. I only felt tired and lonely and my head did ache, but it ached in the way my head always aches. The next morning, on the thirteenth day of October, nine days after we left Kathmandu, each of them spent walking at least ten miles, we walked the two miles to Chyamtang and decided to spend a few days there.

In that long hike the day before from the field full of leeches to our campsite in Chepuwa, I had felt I was negotiating my very existence with each step. But while I spent nine hours all wrapped up in myself, wondering if this plant (*Paris,* for instance) which looked awfully familiar and so much so that it had to be something else, was really itself, wondering if I was seeing something new, and always wondering if I could grow it—and when I realized I could not, I had no interest in the thing before me whatsoever. While I had spent nine hours being a gardener, in other words, Dan and Bleddyn and Sue were gathering seeds. They had collected and recorded the seeds of thirty-nine different plants, among them: *Anemone vitifolia, Rubus lineatus, Cautleya spicata, Paris polyphylla, Schefflera* sp., *Disporum cantoniense, Ari-saema tortuosum, Tricyrtis maculata, Philadelphus tomentosus, Hydrangea anomala, Crawfordia speciosum, Viburnum grandiflorum, Aralia,* and many ferns.

When we reached Chyamtang, we unpacked everything and aired out our clothes and sleeping things. It was a brilliant day of heat and bright light. Dan told me how lucky we were. Apparently, it could have been raining, it could have been cold. I was grateful for all that and grateful too for being able to spend the day lying down and reading and certainly not hiking. It was around then that Sue and I said to each other how hard the whole thing was. Sue came down with a cold. I came down with a case of loss of sense of self, but not only was this not new, I actually enjoy this state and were it not for that, I really would be in a state of loss of sense of self, only I would have no way of knowing so.

All the same, how welcome this day was. A Pause. Sue and I could hardly believe it. Of course, Dan and Bleddyn went off seed hunting or collecting and they expected Sue and me to clean the seed collection from the day before. Sue did her best, I did nothing at all. The day went by.

Chyamtang is way up north in Nepal, not far from the Tibetan border. It seemed to be a big village because many people kept coming and going by us. By many people, I mean perhaps twelve, but we had seen so few people in the last few days that five began to seem like a crowd. They passed through, they stared at Sue and me, and then they went on. At some point we had to take refuge in our tents, she in the one she shared with Bleddyn, I in the one I shared with Dan. A group of children had come by at lunchtime and stared at us as we ate. We grew uncomfortable and went into our tents. While we were in our tents, a large group of people gathered outside and one person would open the tent flap to show us to the other people. We had to call on Sunam, who spoke gruffly to them and made them move away. But nothing made my rest day not blissful. I was reading my book by Frank Smythe about his failed attempt to climb Kanchenjunga in 1930. Three weeks ago I would have had no interest or understanding of his account of climbing a mountain. I knew of him through his writing as a plant hunter. I had no idea that the mountaineer and the plant collector were the same person. Much later, I came to see that he became a plant collector because it was a way for him to climb mountains. His most famous book of plant collecting, *The Valley of Flowers,* is full of the many little side trips he took to climb some summit, insignificant by Himalayan standards but major when compared to the rest of the world's geography. It became clear to me that while trying to climb Everest in the twenties, and then Kanchenjunga in the thirties, the spectacular beauty of a Himalayan spring left such an impression that it either made him a gardener or made him see those mountains as an extension of the garden.

On October 13, our day off, I lay in my tent alone reading. Sue, sick with a cold, dutifully got up and cleaned the seeds that Bleddyn and Dan had collected. I wasn't very interested in this since none would survive in my garden. Dan had gone off in the direction of a village north of us, a village called Ritak, which Sunam said bordered Tibet and so he warned us against going there. Dan went off toward it just the same and said he would be careful not to wander into Tibet. Bleddyn had gone back toward Chepuwa. On this side of Chepuwa both he and Dan had seen a gulley that went up into a thickly forested area, and they were both sure that it was rich in pleasingly ornamental flower-bearing plants. That night, over dinner, they went back and forth regarding what to do, should they both go back to it or should they both go up to Ritak? Dan wanted to go to Ritak and so he did. Bleddyn went back toward Chepuwa and collected in the gulley above it. Dan went out of Chyamtang, crossed the Arun, walked on its banks for a quarter of a mile or so, and then re-crossed it on a bridge made of bamboo. At that point of its life, the Arun is closer to its source than when we first saw it in Tumlingtar. Near Tumlingtar, it is broad and majestic and even calm and forgiving, flowing in a dreamy way, making you long for a swim, lulling you into any kind of romantic thoughts you can have about calm and steady flowing water. But up near its source, it is fierce, roaring, as if trying to escape from an eternal dam. I had never seen water like that, so clear, so translucent, yet thick like a cloud. It looked as if you could see through it, but you couldn't. Rushing furiously, scouring the earth, it was ready to take with it anything that stood in its path. To see this force, at that juncture about twenty feet wide and I do not know how deep, bridged by a structure made of bamboo, is among the most alarming things I have ever seen in my life. All of the other most alarming things I have seen in my life occurred not far from there. Dan crossed this bridge and went up to Ritak.

The climb up to Ritak was steep, Dan said. When he got to the village some people mistook him for a doctor

Bamboo bridge crossing a tributary of the Arun

and asked him to come and take care of a man who Dan could see was near death. He didn't know what was wrong with the man but he thought it might be some kind of cancer. Anyway, he left some Advil and tried to tell them he was not a doctor. Returning to Chyamtang at the end of the day, as he crossed the river over the bamboo bridge, without him knowing it, some boys had followed him. Suddenly, when he was midpoint on the bridge, the part of the journey over any bridge when you feel most vulnerable, the bridge began to shake and sway. Frightened, of course, he didn't know which way to run, but then he heard some laughing and looked to see these boys jumping up and down on the Ritak side of the bridge. He arrived in camp at around half past three, looking exhausted. He had just seen a man dying and for a moment, on that bridge, he thought he was dying too. Not long after that Bleddyn returned too with a bounty of things, more than Dan had found in Ritak but with no encounters with other human beings. We all went to the little stream that was a quarter of a mile away and washed ourselves and our clothes, for suddenly it had been decided that we should take another rest day. It seemed that there were some valleys and ridges above us that the plant collectors wanted to explore.

Dinner that night was wonderful even though it was the same as all the nights before: soup, potatoes, rice and dahl, or noodles, one or other, sometimes all of them. It seemed as if all the people living in the area had descended on our camp and were just sitting and looking at us. It was as if we were a living cinema. They watched us eat and talk. Sometimes they peered at me and said things about me to Sunam, but of course when I asked him what they were saying, he suddenly did not understand the local language. One woman did make me understand that she thought I was wearing a mask, that my face was not my real face. She strangely, I thought, bore a strong physical resemblance to my own mother, who had been dead three years then. We saw a beautiful girl, who seemed perhaps eleven years old, perhaps thirteen, we couldn't tell. She had just returned from tending a field about two thousand feet above us. We could tell this because she was wearing a beautiful primrose, blue, in her hair. Dan and Bleddyn kept trying to identify it. It was a primrose that bloomed in the fall, so they were not likely to find any seed for it.

In my sleeping bag at last, I fell asleep without worry for the first time in a week, without worrying that I would slip out of the sleeping bag and tent and fall down some ledge, for it was the first time since we left Num that we were camped on level ground; without worrying about leeches, without worrying about Maoists. It never ceased to amaze me how uneven the landscape was. A distance of a city block meant going up or going down, and though Dan, especially Dan, and Bleddyn took to it very well, the extremely uneven terrain was trying for Sue and me. I complained bitterly to myself, and quarreled with the ground as I trod on it, but even then I knew I was having the very most wonderful time of my life, that I would never forget what I was doing, that I would long to see again every inch of the ground that I was walking on the minute I turned my back on it. At around one o'clock that morning I came out of the tent to pee and met a black sky full of stars. Everyone was asleep, everything was quiet, once again I was struck at how far away I was from all that was truly familiar to me, but I didn't long for anything; I felt quite lost and this feeling led to another feeling—happiness.

A third day of rest was called for and it coincided with the decision to explore the valleys above us. From Ritak, Dan had been able to see a forested ridge above Chyamtang and he thought if we could go above that, we would find things even I could grow. Bleddyn and Dan then argued over the way to get there. Dan had seen Bleddyn's suggested route from Ritak, and since he did not like heights and did not like traveling along narrow ledges, he had ruled it out. Of course if he had been told that ripe fruit of the most unusual primrose or peony was to be had at the end of the most narrow ledge in the world, he would have lost his dislike for high, narrow ledges immediately. Also from Ritak, he had been able to see that the ledge ended and dropped off into nothing, empty air, not a route that led up above them. Sunam then made some inquiries and found a man who said that he knew most certainly of a way up from the ledge to the forests above. We took a lunch and with the man guiding us, Dan, Bleddyn, and I started out for the ledge itself, which was an hour's walk up from our camp. I could soon see what Dan objected to. It was a narrow path, hardly big enough for one person, certainly it would be difficult to pass another person without their cooperation. I walked along clinging to the granite walls of the mountain, trying hard not to look down at the sheer nothing on the other side of me. The ledge took turns curving around so that we could not see what was coming and then jutting out so that we could see all too clearly how it snaked up. Still it was full of plants in seed, none of which would be hardy enough for me to grow, most of them mysterious, most of them new to me. But it was no place for the leisureliness of collecting, from Dan's point of view, and so he and I turned back to camp, picked up Thile Sherpa, and set off for the same forests above Chyamtang but from another direction. That day, we walked up to ten thousand feet, the highest we had walked up in our nine days of walking. We crossed open sunbaked meadows, through deeply shaded and moist areas; we went down and up, but mostly it was up. Once when emerging from a forested area, I looked back and saw in the not too far distance, a gleaming white pyramid floating above the green-clad mountaintops that surrounded it. Kanchenjunga, I was told it was, the third-highest mountain the world, and it was less than twenty miles away. Each night before I fell asleep in my tent, I read Frank Smythe's wonderful account of the failed attempt to climb this mountain in 1930, and among the thrills of reading it was becoming familiar with some people and a terrain between the pages of his book and outside the book, this at the same time. To now see this mountain that I had never paid attention to before I came to Nepal, so nearby, looking as if someone had just now placed it there a minute ago, left me openmouthed, in awe. I made Dan take a picture of me with it in the background, and when we started walking again, I kept looking back at it as if I was afraid I would never see it again. And I never did see it again, for when we came back down a great mass of clouds hid it from view, as they did for the rest of my time there. We saw blooming along the banks of the many streams we crossed the same beautiful primrose that we had seen decorating a girl's hair but there weren't any with seed. In that area, above Chyamtang, Dan and Bleddyn collected the seeds of so many things: *Vaccinium, Anemone,* another primrose, *Thalictrum, Smilacina, Begonia oalmatumeuonymus, Codonopsis,* clematis (species and *Montana*), *Cardiocrinum, Gaultheria, Arisaema, Clerodendron* (in many places its red fruit reigned dominant), *Hypericum, Delphinium stapeliosmum, Rhododendron arboreum, Ophiopogon intermedius, Ligularia fisheri, Strobilanthes* sp., *Begonia* sp., *Jasminum humile, Sarcococca hookeriana, Pleurospermum* sp., *Cotoneaster microphylus, Gaultheria fragrantissima, Clematis* sp., *Holboellia latifolia, Meconopsis nepaulensis, Aconitum tuberosum, Rodgersia nepaulensis, Aralia cachemirica, Sorbus cuspidata, Roscoea auriculata, Hydrangea*

Author posing against the peaks of Kanchenjunga

sp., *Polygonatum cirrhifolium, Zanthoxylum nepalense,*
Hedychium sp., *Lyonia* sp., among many others, just to
name some of them, but I was not so very interested
because almost none of it would thrive in my garden, as
Dan mockingly pointed out to me.

Returning to camp, I did not see Kanchenjunga, but
I enjoyed all the same the novelty of seeing a way I had
come going in the other direction. On my journey, there
was no coming and going, I was always going somewhere and everything I saw, I saw only from one direction, which was going forward, going toward, and then
I was going away. So often I read in Frank Smythe's *The
Kanchenjunga Adventure,* of him going from a camp at
one altitude to the other, and I came to see how com-
forting this back and forth in a strange place could be.
It seems to me a natural impulse to begin to think of
every place in which you find yourself for longer than
a day as home, and to make it familiar. Dan and I descended more than twice as quickly as we had ascended,
practically greeting the path as it wound through forest,
pasture, over steep mounds, dividing a roar of water as
it rushed to meet up eventually with the great Arun.
How happy we were to see our tents there in the middle
of the village, the only flat place for miles around, the
only flat place until the next village, which was miles
away. Cook had made a special dinner of rice with a spe-

cial dahl and a cake even, but I couldn't eat anything. I felt sick and so went to bed right away, and was asleep by eight. Much singing and carrying on was done late into the night, Dan said, by Sunam, Mingma, and Thile, and the porters. I awoke at two o'clock in the morning to silence and crept outside for my nightly pee. So soft everything was, in the blue-gray moonlight, the moon no longer completely full; how permeable the landscape looked, as if I could just walk through the hills and the trees, walk through them, not over them, as if they would yield.

In the morning we packed. We felt refreshed. We were beginning anew. We said goodbye to Chyamtang and it almost seemed like an act of rebellion or liberation. We were moving on. One of our porters, a fourteen-year-old boy named Jhaba Lama, came from this village. It was so fortuitous that when Sunam was hiring porters in Tumlingtar that Jhaba was there and was only returning home, not looking for work at all, and here was a job that would bring him to his home. The part of Nepal we were traveling in was not the part usually taken on a trek. Trekking paths usually make their way to a base camp at one of the high summits or around one of the nature-preserve areas attached to one of the high summits. So how fortunate for Jhaba that the path that would lead us to flowers went through his village. He was only fourteen, the same age as my son, Harold, and perhaps because I missed Harold so, I immediately singled him out for kind attention. When I told Sunam how touched I was by his presence, this little boy, the same age as my son, carrying sixty-pound loads strapped up on his back, he said of course I would be touched because Jhaba was a Sherpa. He did look like the people who come from Tibet. One day, when Jhaba had carried my bags, out of the blue I gave him a one-thousand-rupee note and I told him not to tell his fellow porters. When we arrived in Chyamtang, he went immediately to visit his family. That afternoon, his mother came to visit the camp and she brought us eggs and vegetables from her garden. She was a very beautiful woman with the same warm brown eyes as his, small and elegant. Sunam, who that time could understand her dialect, said that she thanked us for being kind to her son. Now, as we were leaving Chyamtang, we passed by Jhaba's house and he wanted us to meet his father, who was a lama. It was clear they were an important family for their house was larger than the others and they seemed more prosperous in general. His father wore a long orange silk robe and had the general air of someone who spent most of the day reading and thinking about things judged to be important. He and Jhaba's mother, whom we had already met, greeted us with just the right amount of warmth and distance. They made us wish we had met them earlier and so had seen them more, and yet they also made us feel that this was enough. I told them how wonderful their son was and, according to Sunam, they agreed and also said that their son did not like studying. We said our goodbyes and started on our way, down, down, down, on our way to crossing the Arun River for the last time. In Chyamtang we had been at 7,260 feet altitude. When we left the village that morning at half past seven it was seventy-seven degrees Fahrenheit. We crossed the Arun for the last time at an altitude of 5,620 feet. It was the highest point for a crossing we made of this river.

TWO DAYS TO THUDAM

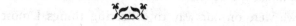

Those three days off had renewed us. It is true Dan and Bleddyn had gathered a lot of seeds, but they wouldn't have gone out of their way to make this collection, what they had collected is the sort of thing you collect on your way to real garden treasure. Bleddyn and Sue, gardeners and nursery people from as ideal a situation as can be in the temperate region of the prosperous world, Wales, were more enthusiastic about collecting in this area than Dan and me. But even among Dan and me there was some variance in satisfaction. Dan, as a nurseryman, has customers in various gardening zones. The collection of seeds he made the day before, when he and I went out together, would be good for some of his customers. He often collects in Chile and Guatemala, and when I see these things listed in his catalogue I simply move on. I know something native to Guatemala or to Chile will only last in Vermont if grown in a clay pot. And it was so with almost everything that we collected above Chyamtang. I could grow it in a pot or as an annual, the begonia, the *Strobilanthes*, the *Osbeckia*. Now we were on our way to collecting things I most definitely would be able to grow in my garden zone of USDA 5. At various times we walked by men, and they did not look at us. They seemed very absorbed by the reality of their lives and we were not part of it. We crossed the swaying bridge. Half a mile or so from this was the bamboo bridge where Dan had the frightening experience, and he took us to it. We naturally had our pictures taken at the approximate spot where Dan had been when the naughty boys had scared him. We then began the walk up, for to get to our desire—beautiful plants native to the Himalaya but that will grow happily in Vermont or somewhere like that—requires climbing high. The higher we got the hotter the sun. How glad I was to come upon a place where the now familiar marriage trees, the two *Ficus (Ficus benghalensis* and *Ficus religiosa)*, were growing. Sue and I rested. Dan and Bleddyn had rested there perhaps fifteen minutes ago;

they were, as usual, ahead of us. Three miles or so away from Chyamtang we had lunch, but it might as well have been ten hundred times that distance, for the night before seemed so long ago. The constant roar or sight of the Arun was no longer there. And the other thing was that the mountains, or the hills, or whatever they should properly be called, were no longer far away. We were now really in them. The landscape suddenly began to close in on us. When we began our trek so many days ago, Sunam would point out to me some snowcapped mountains in the distance that were shielding from my sight our destination. Now the shield itself was behind me, I could no longer see the mountains that had been the shield of my destination. If before I had not wondered if I was walking on the ledges of the world, now the thought would most certainly have occurred to me. We walked along the edges of some deceptively gentle sloping cliffs but any misstep would have sent us rolling down to the bottom of a ravine. Sometimes we were in the open and sometimes in thick forests of bamboo and maple, and all the time collecting *Thalictrum, Lilium,* impatiens, a species of *Roscoea, Clematis connata, Deutzia,* and the yellow-flowered climbing *Dicentra.* The forested places were the most wonderful for collecting from my point of view, for I began to see my garden again. Here suddenly we were walking on a carpet of the fallen leaves of *Magnolia campbellii,* and looking up I saw that I was in the thick of them and a hunt for fruits began. We found many fruits lying on the ground but most of their seeds were rotten. But growing in this area was *Paris,* and Dan and Bleddyn had found a form that was variegated in leaf. That was new to them and caused much excitement. But they had not found a plant with ripe seed, that is seed worth collecting, so in a frenzy we all began to look for more of this *Paris* with seed. None could be found. Perhaps among the most annoying things to me all along was that I could only identify plants that were already familiar to me; and then again, sometimes when confronted with a plant I knew really well before, when seeing it in a place that was new to me, I found it mysterious and foreign. And so while joining in the search for the new *Paris,* the one with the distinctly variegated leaves, everything I saw before me was a mystery and so therefore not important. When, in that moment, I came upon some fruits of *Magnolia campbellii,* its appearance familiar to me because it resembles the fruits of other magnolias, it seemed to me completely weird, unrecognizable; I remember my brain trying desperately to make sense of it, trying desperately to find a similar image stored so that the soggy, rotting, cucumberlike pods that littered the area around me would lead to some pronouncement of recognition. It

was with a sense of despair and resignation at not knowing what was in front of me that I said to Dan, "What
is this?" and I was pointing to the much sought after
variegated *Paris,* bearing a handful of fruit.

Dan and Bleddyn, at this moment two of the most
experienced plant hunters in the entire world, were a
sight. All our days before, going up and down, meeting
the Maoists, placating them, avoiding them, resting for
a couple of days in the high-mountain heat, had turned
out to be an ordeal for them. What they wanted was to
be in the middle of a forest that had the widest selection
of gardenworthy plants. What they wanted was to collect the seeds of plants that would make a gardener like
me, someone who wanted to know about and be
engaged with the world but in the most benign way
possible, excited. I have made a garden in a part of the
world where the flora is interesting and full of wonder
enough. I only have to turn to a page in the travels of
William Bartram and there I will find any number of
plants (red bud, fringe tree, tulip tree) that enthrall me.
But something that never escapes me as I putter about
the garden, physically and mentally: desire and curiosity
inform the inevitable boundaries of the garden, and
boundaries, especially when they are an outgrowth of
something as profound as the garden with all its holy
restrictions and admonitions, must be violated. The

story of the garden, when it is told by the gardener, is an homage to the gardener's curiosity and explanation of a transgression by a transgressor.

Sue and I never could keep up with them, they were always at least a mile ahead, in search of whatever would yield up seeds. But this new area was so interesting to them that they lingered in it. They found *Paris* in its regular form and then, unexpectedly, they found it in a form they had never heard of, they found a form with variegated leaves. The leaves of this plant, *Paris,* are usually just the color of leaves, green, but the one they found had white streaks and through their experienced eyes they could see that this was not from some deficiency in the individual plant itself; they could see that this was a natural deviation. They were excited. They were very excited. They shouted out to Sue and me, that there was a variegated *Paris* in this area and if we found one with good seed we would be rewarded. All along, I was so amazed at my very presence in this very place, I was so keenly aware of how ignorant I was in every way of the world in which I was in. I was in the forest but all the trees looked the same and none of them seemed familiar even though some of them I had growing in my own garden in Vermont. I was tumbling about in a tangle of fear, suspicion, and ignorance when suddenly as clear as a newly learnt letter in the alphabet I saw the variegated *Paris* that they were looking for, the plant, at that moment, they desired so.

When I declaimed, "What is this?" for by then it was a declamation, I was so ignorant and because of that I was always saying "What is this?" and it went from a genuine innocent question to a whine. "What is this?" came my voice, and I could feel my companions, Dan, Bleddyn, Sue, recoil, my voice being no longer associated with human curiosity but a human dolefulness, something dull and tired, even reproachful. But this time in the forest, under a canopy of *Magnolia campbellii* and oak and maples, with perhaps the desired variegated *Paris* hidden somewhere, when I said, "What is this?" both Bleddyn and Dan leapt to the place where I pointed my walking stick, the very one I had many days ago bought in Kathmandu. Dan arrived there first, identified the plant as the much sought *Paris* with variegated foliage, and a magnificent display of black seeds bursting out of a vivid red fleshy matter. He plucked it and put it in a plastic bag, the very kind I would use to pack my son, Harold, a sandwich for his school lunch. They found a few other plants of *Paris* like this to make them understand it was something new, but it also made them look back into their memory of other plant hunters', their contemporaries', accounts of the *Paris*. They wondered if they had found something new. They believed they had found something new. They doubted they had found something new. And then they were very happy that this *Paris* was new to them.

We walked on and I saw *Lilium nepalense,* among other things, in seed. We walked and walked and then finally, at around four o'clock we came to camp. Somehow Sunam had found a clearing where there was an abandoned building made of stone, wood, and mud and a stream. Our cook seemed happy by this, but how could I really know? Our campsite looked awfully like the leech field of many nights before, but we were too high and it was too cold for them. I certainly was happy about this. That night Sunam gave back to me my satellite telephone and I called my son, Harold, and now as I write this I do not ask him if our conversation seemed unreal, unexpected, and frightening, but so it seemed to me then. We were in the open air under a sky that seemed domed, curving into a horizon that was not so far away. I had no appetite and could not eat. I went to bed at about seven o'clock and tried to read my Frank Smythe but could not. I fell asleep and woke up from dreaming that I was sliding out of my tent down toward a precipice, which was far away. That dream was not too far from the real, for I awoke at around midnight to find myself, feet first, sliding out of the tent. We were, as usual, camping on ground that sloped downward more than not, and the higher up we went that would be so.

The mornings were really cold, the now not-so-distant tops of ever-higher-heights covered with fresh snow, but by the time we were ready to leave at quarter to seven, it had warmed up to sixty-five degrees Fahrenheit. We left camp as if it was a new experience, as if we had just begun the journey to find plants that we loved and could grow in the many gardens in our imaginations. That morning, the porters were singing and they seemed to have stayed up most of the night singing. We wanted to ask Sunam if they were singing because they were happy but we guessed he would tell us yes, they were singing because they were happy, just as if we had asked him if they were singing because they were unhappy, he would tell us yes. We knew him as well as that after walking with him for more than ten days now.

Dan kept saying that today we were going to Thudam. He kept talking about Thudam and after not knowing anything about our other destinations, the village or city or town of Thudam became practically magical and even mythical. I can't wait to get to Thudam, he kept saying. I had known of Thudam through the book *A Plantsman in Nepal* written by the great plantsman Roy Lancaster. That and a similar volume he wrote about plant collecting in China are two of the most important books in the canon of modern plant collecting, and any amateur interested in this area of the garden will only be pleased with the encouragement and pleasure that is to be found in them. Lancaster's name came up often among the plantsmen. Bleddyn, for one, was very disappointed when we did not get a chance to go looking up the Barun Valley. Lancaster had found some wonderful and rare thing growing there, and he said no one had gone to look for plants there since.

This singing of the porters and Dan's excitement about Thudam began to make Thudam seem the hot spot of this part of the world. Somehow, an idea got stuck in our heads, not from Lancaster, by then I couldn't remember exactly what he had said about Thudam, that Thudam would offer us a memorable view of life here. For one thing, from there was a road that led directly into Tibet and people from Tibet came there to trade things. We were hoping that the day we arrived would be a market day. To Thudam then, it was. Walking that day along the usual narrow path, in which it would be impossible for two people to walk along together side by side, concentrating hard so that I did not fall into the many yawning chasms that were a natural accompaniment to the path, I felt gloriously happy. Everywhere there was something that even I could see was worth collecting. The bounty included: *Hydrangea robusta,* a species of *Lobelia, Rhododendron arboreum* subsp. *cinnamomeum* (this was a rhododendron with peeled bark like cinnamon, or like the bark of *Acer griseum*), *Meconopsis villosa, Arisaema propinquuum, Rhododendron bureavii, Acer campbellii,* and the much desired *Daphne bholua.* Twice, at two different times, Sunam tapped me on the shoulder and asked me to look over my shoulder, and once I saw a stark white pyramid set against the bluest of skies: that, he said, was Makalu. The next time I saw part of stark white jutting, it was farther away and looked more like a series of pyramids joined together: that, he said, was Kanchenjunga. When we rounded a bend, clambering up and over a series of boulders, he said I would not see them in that way again. At midday we stopped for lunch at a waterfall, a fierce gush of water screaming down the mountain, dashing itself into a natural basin, and we enjoyed sitting in it and cooling ourselves off. The day had gotten hot and the heat as always seemed new and unexpected.

✖

It was in the afternoon that we really started to go up and would not go down below six thousand feet for days again. Sometimes, I had to get down on my hands and knees to crawl across a part of the path that the porters, carrying our luggage, not to mention our dining table and four chairs, had nimbly maneuvered. It was that afternoon that I saw rhododendrons that were not shrubs but trees thirty feet tall. And it was then I saw the one with the cinnamon bark and it was a revelation. The rhododendron in general is perhaps the most misused flowering shrub in an American garden. It is planted near a house, often to hide the hideous but appropriate material that is the foundation for a building. They come in perfect colors—purple, pink, violet—and they bloom with generosity, in thrusts. But these qualities, the abundance in color and bloom, plus the ease with which they often can be grown, make them taken for granted to the point of abuse. To see them now, then, to see a rhododendron, with a trunk as thick as a pine and thirty feet tall, and with leaves almost as long as my lower arm, was as magical as seeing the mountain Makalu from a distance. I walked along in a state of complete wonder for I was in a forest made up of these plants—rhododendron with peeling bark, and maple and bamboo. At around nine thousand feet we came upon a stupa and some prayer flags and rested. Then we made a turn going decidedly away from where we had just come and started going down, losing a thousand feet in altitude, going toward Thudam.

We passed no one other than people in our own party. Above us were huge boulders, and I couldn't help but wonder what kept them in place. Ordinarily, I never question the ground I am on but in this place of determined verticals, everything seemed delicately perched, waiting for the day when it would come tumbling down. What if that day happened to be the moment when I was just passing by?

Toward Thudam we walked, and Sunam said it was just down there, and whenever we got just down there, Thudam was beyond that. Beneath were narrow rock-strewn valleys that would then become open and vast. We walked along open, exposed ledges and then suddenly it was dark and cold and we were in a forest, and so Sunam said we would spend the night there. We camped in a forest of *Rhododendron hodgsonii,* surrounded by them, towering above us, right next to a waterfall that was really a point of relief for a more powerful waterfall that was nearby. But the smaller outlet had a roar all its own and it dominated the realm of sleep to such a degree that we all agreed we had never slept better. We left camp the next morning at half past seven. It was forty-eight degrees Fahrenheit and we were at an altitude of 9,930 feet. It was dark when we had made camp the night before, and we had not realized we were in the middle of the path, the middle of the road as it was. Suddenly, a herd of cows and their herder were coming our way. I recognized the herder as the same one we had seen days ago just at the time of the leech field when we were trying to avoid the Maoists. And this made me understand that while each day had seemed new and separate not continuous with the day before, for some people, for the people living there, life, each day, was connected into one whole. And I say this as if it were new and I say this with complete familiarity.

To Thudam then, it would be on this day. We walked on and then by ten o'clock that morning we were in Thudam. We could see it from a distance. It was a collection of small brown flat-roofed houses made of wood, perhaps even wood from some of the forests we had just walked through. It was the very opposite of a market town or of bustling anything. From it, a trail went straight up toward Tibet and a pass called Umbak Bhanjyang. I saw a man carrying a large load of something on his back and going up that way. When we got to the village we saw no one out- side. Inside the main building, Sunam bought a large quantity of rice. We wondered if there was anything we might purchase, just as mementos, so that long after all this was hard to believe, we would have some little thing to reassure us that yes, one day, we had been in Thudam, a little village in northeast Nepal, up near the Tibetan border. Dan bought some aprons, worn by women there as part of their daily dress, and some yak herd bells. There was nothing else for sale. Disappointed at the absence of a Thudam metropolis, we crossed the river that separated it from the rest of our journey. And that river! It was a confluence of water rushing down from many places above us. Its color was an unfiltered blue, and I guessed that it was glacial in origin, the cold melt of something that had been frozen for an eternity. We crossed it, me haphazardly; the bridge was made up of some logs tied together with a thick twine. I fell off it into the water once. The water was cold, but not unbearably so.

When we departed from Thudam, I was almost in a state of disbelief. I kept looking back to make sure I had really been in such a place, that the place called Thudam did exist. I had been there. I had tried to buy some little knickknack, some little souvenir that I would later look at to provide me with certainty that I had been to Thudam. But there wasn't anything to buy. I did have for a meal some of the rice Sunam bought there. A bend in the path and I could no longer even see it, the collection of brown flat-roofed houses among boulders the size of the houses themselves. It was when looking back that I saw a small specter heading toward the road to Tibet. It was Bleddyn, and he had taken a wrong turn. In that vast landscape, destinations are few

Remote outpost of Thudam, on the Tibetan border

but the opportunities to make a wrong turn are many. We called to him but he could not hear us and eventually a porter ran back all that way, a mile or so, to fetch him. A mile or two at ten thousand feet altitude is no ordinary mile.

We sat in the shade after that and had lunch at about half past eleven. Without meaning to, I sat on some precious *Aconitum,* but since it was not in flower, I did not care. While eating, Dan and Bleddyn cleaned seeds, labeled and numbered the collections. It was seventy-three degrees Fahrenheit and we were at an altitude of 11,670 feet. None of us felt the effects of the high altitude, except that we never felt like eating. The sky was free of clouds, the air not hot, just brilliantly clear. Then suddenly, a wind came up, the sun vanished, and we could tell that we mustn't linger. We set off again. I began to see, for the first time and in abundance, the species of *Meconopsis grandis* and it had seed. I, of course, had never seen it in flower, but I began to recognize the leaves, narrow, hairy, and long, growing straight up, with the dried scapes sticking out. We were now walking along the stony banks of a fierce glass-bottom blue river. It came rushing from somewhere deep in the mountains toward which we were heading. The bank on the other side was thick with rhododendrons, shorter ones, which Bleddyn said were *R. campanulatum.* They were like rhododendrons I was used to seeing, their leaves, a normal leaf shape, not big and broad and reminding me of something else. They were in full sun and grew thickly, as if to make a deep hedge. I could only imagine how amazing they would be in springtime, all in bloom.

The path opened up now, but it was not really a path, not a path as I knew it. Nothing was as I knew it to be, this was true. The path became a wide open pasture of boulders perched on top of each other and we were just stepping from one to the other. Each step was a balancing act, each step called for a different kind of concentration than the kind required when we were walking in file in the forest. We were in an Alpine landscape, not a meadow, not a scree, just a great big expanse of rocks with low-growing juniper growing around them and some low-growing rhododendron spreading out forever and ever like an eternal carpet, berberis and then more rhododendron, taller than the carpet-growing one, but lots of that also, the *Meconopsis grandis* and *paniculata,* and some woody *Potentilla.* The wind grew harder and then it began to rain and sleet, and then finally snow. I suddenly found myself all alone in a boulder-strewn valley and I couldn't quite tell how the terrain went from being a river valley to a series of streams, each of them leading to some new direction.

Every step I took seemed to lead me to some new vista, some new path, and when I looked backward to see where I had come from, I did not recognize what I saw. Above me were huge boulders, all of them again seemed delicately perched, ready to come down on me. The path I followed crossed a gully, then traversed a series of streams then followed along a larger stream. Everywhere were rocks, large boulders, streams, the air streaked with sleet and snow, and it was growing darker. I was afraid I was lost. I called Sunam but when I realized that I could hardly hear my own voice, I stopped doing that. Without knowing anything else to do, I persisted along the banks of the largest of the thick blue streams. I came upon our camp and I realized just how frightened I had been. I would not ever have been lost, Sunam would not have allowed that to happen. That night Sunam had Cook make for us a dish from his region of Nepal, a nice thick stew with dumplings, potatoes, carrots, turnips, and peas. It was delicious but I could not eat it. I drank some tea and went to bed. It was cold but I had the brilliant idea of filling up our drinking-water bottles, the ones we carried with us during the day, with hot water and placing them in my sleeping bag next to me. I slept until midnight when, on going outside for a pee, I met a beautiful, cold, clear starry night and a good six inches of snow on the ground. In the morning we had noodle soup for breakfast, another specialty from Sunam's region, and then we headed up to the pass of Jangla Bhanjyang, and over to the even more mythical and magical Topke Gola. It is among the places in the world plantsmen live for.

TOPKE GOLA

That night in the cold dark and snow when I had stumbled into camp, what I had missed seeing growing spectacularly among the boulders hovering above me was the great *Rheum nobile*, growing solitary, erect, aloof, and stiff like little sentinels. It was fall and they had long passed their bloom beauty, and so even now I would never see them in their true blooming glory. And why was I so awestruck to see it? I had never before seen it growing anyway. As far as I know, it cannot be found in any garden, certainly not in the garden of anyone I would know. In my life as a gardener, there have been a number of plants I have wanted to see, for the sheer unbelievableness of them: the blue poppy (*Meconopsis benticifolia*), *Gunnera manticata* (for its, literally, giant-sized leaves), just to name two of them. The *Rheum nobile* has been among them. I first saw the blue poppy many years ago growing in a display at the Chelsea Flower Show in England. My true delight and surprise proved very embarrassing to the people observing me; and I could not tell whether it was my ignorance or my enthusiasm. The *Gunnera* I saw in a garden out in the Pacific Northwest. That time, no one witnessed my delight and surprise. The *Rheum nobile* will only be found in books written by plant hunters and only ones who have been to certain areas of the Himalaya. There is a picture of it in flower to be found in *Flowers of the Himalaya* by Oleg Polunin and Adam Stainton. It is, as usual, solitary, growing in stark, rocky mountainsides, way above the tree line and surrounded by *Meconopsis* and some kinds of *Primula*. Its true flowers are hidden beneath large creamy yellow bracts—that are almost as big as its large leaves—and it stands around three feet high. What I was looking at then was its dried-up self full of seed. But neither Bleddyn nor Dan wanted to collect them because the conditions under which it will agree to bloom do not exist in an American or English garden. Bleddyn said that he had never even heard of anyone being able to make seeds of it germinate. It was while looking at the brown, dried sentinel, standing all alone among rocks, that I thought of the description Joseph Hooker made about this *Rheum*: "On the black rocks the gigantic rhubarb forms pale pyramidal towers a yard high, of inflated reflexed bracts, that conceal the flowers, and overlapping one another like tiles, protect them from wind and rain: a whorl of broad green leaves edged with red spreads on the ground at the base of the plant, contrasting in color with the transparent bracts, which are yellow, margined with pink. This is the handsomest herbaceous plant in Sikkim." He was describing it in bloom. At first I saw only one dried sentinel and then as my eyes grew accustomed to the landscape, they appeared frequently enough but always somewhat far apart from each other.

The wonderful sighting of the *R. nobile* soon gave way to other things. It was near twenty degrees Fahrenheit when we left camp and crossed the blue, cold river along which banks we had spent the night. We were now heading to Topke Gola. We were in a rocky valley and going up. As usual, what seemed from a distance to be a point of termination, that is, the end of the road, was just another opening on to another vista. The boulders got bigger as we went up and the valley opened up wider too. We were now in the middle also of many

Author and Thile Sherpa beside a Tibetan Rhubarb plant, Rheum nobile

rivulets, streams, tricklings of water burbling up and coming down. There were no trees here, just shrubby potentillas and junipers. The *R. nobile* was everywhere and so was another uncollectible, a plant called *Saussurea*. I had seen pictures of it, but before this, it held no interest to me. And now I understood why. The one I saw (and there are many others) was a white hairy mound, sprawled among the brown rocks and against a background of a very high snowcapped peak. So too we found other species of *Meconopsis* (*discigera* and *bella*) and primrose *(stuartii), Rhodiola, Saxifraga (parnassifolia), Pleurospermum,* lily *(nanum), Geranium (nakonianum).*

Left to ourselves, we would have been lost in this sea of rocks and boulders, for this landscape was as familiar to me as the one on Mars. Every obvious way to the pass that would then lead us to Topke Gola was the wrong path, and it was only thanks to Sunam, who whenever the going was difficult always brought up the rear, and the rear was Sue and especially me and my difficulties. And my difficulties were these: I found each plant, each new turn in the road, each new turn in the weather, from cold to hot and then back again, each new set of boulders so absorbing, so new, and the newness so absorbing, and I was so in need of an explanation for each thing, that I was often in tears, troubling myself with questions, such as what am I and what is the thing in front of me.

More than a few people have gone beyond the boundaries of the earth's atmosphere and on returning, participate in parades and festivals and ceremonies with joy and enthusiasm. They have made the unknown normal-seeming immediately. It is just as well that none of these people were me. Had I been the first person to walk on the surface of the moon, I don't think I would be able to speak for one hundred years afterward. As it is, I just went to Nepal on a plant-hunting, seed-collecting trek and the landscape at the foothills of the Himalayan mountains have left my tongue somewhat stilled, perhaps permanently so.

If someone had not shown me the correct path to go over the pass, I would not have found it by myself. I started up and it seemed friendly enough. I could still make out some growing things, the *Saussurea* was there, some gentian, and then much snow. I was now in that far distance that I could see from Num (at least the snow-covered peaks). I walked up and the snow got deep and icy and slippery. Of course, the top to the pass was farther than I thought, and the snow got deeper as I went up. The sun shone brightly and the light from the reflection was practically blinding. Halfway up, I could hear the sound of bells, and then soon a herd of yaks and their herder came into view. I had to make way for them, stepping out of the path, while at the same time making sure not to fall off into some bottomless depth that seemed ever nearby. I stood still, on the side as they passed, and then regained the path, only to hear the same sound of a caravan of yaks coming toward me again. This happened two more times and in a way they were a marvelous distraction. The herds were about seven yaks each, and each yak was decorated with bells and strings of wool dyed red, or white. The herders accompanying the yaks seemed not to notice us, or to pay any special attention to us. They did not look like any of the people I had seen before. They did not look like anyone we had met below the altitude of Thudam. From speaking to them, Sunam learned that they were carrying corn to Tibet and would return with rice and salt.

At the very top of the pass I stopped for a rest. It had taken us two hours to walk up to the pass and it had been a struggle for me. We were at an altitude of 15,600 feet. I felt exhausted, physically of course, but that I could handle. It was just that I felt emotionally so. I rested at the stupa, for there was one; and there were prayer flags too. There is the proper way to go around one, it is to the right; but I long ago could not understand what was the right way or the wrong way and I only hoped that the god of this place would look kindly on my ignorance, which only came from exhaustion. Sunam pointed out to me where I had just walked up and then he showed me something, a lake, a hidden lake that could only be seen from the pass. It was so unexpected, so pristine, so real and yet not so, that I felt as if I would dissolve. I did not. I made Dan take a picture of me with it in the background, and I do not know whether it was in consolation or confirmation that he told me the water in the lake eventually found its way to the Ganges.

Leaving the pass was like leaving a great book, which had yielded every kind of satisfaction that is to be found in a great book, except that with such a book you can immediately begin on page one again and create the feeling of not having read it before, even though the reality is you have read it before. How I wanted reaching the pass, going up to it and then leaving it behind, to be something like that, the reading of a great book, the texture of it, the rocks moving under my feet, the flowers that I could never cultivate all full of collectible seed, the precariously standing boulders, each one looking as if it was just about to roll down on top of me and only me; the six-inch deep snow, the slipping around in it and falling down at least once, the clearest of blue skies above me, the sun hot even though I was in the midst of cold and snow, the herd of yaks, the hidden lake, seen by so very few human eyes for all of its millions of years' existence, its contents eventually joining

Author and Dan Hinkley on the high pass between Thudam and Topke Gola

up with the great Ganges. To make the experience like a book, here it is in a book I am writing now for myself. But it is very hard to do this, for each word I put in the book is a word I have had to part with, each experience I portray in this book is one I had to part with. I have not wanted to part with anything, word or experience, I have had while walking around the foothills of the Himalaya in Nepal among its flowers. The book I am writing and so therefore reading will soon be taken away from me. The chances of me going over that pass and seeing that lake hidden just below it again are practically nil. I shall go looking for seeds again and I shall go somewhere else.

I walked down on the other side of the pass and it seemed to me not a mirror image of what I had just come up. But perhaps this experience was determined by my knees. Going up is hard on the lungs, going down is hard on the knees. I saw nothing growing on the way down for some time. The fact that the caravan of herders and yaks had an hour or so before been on the very path I was now on seemed unreal to me. There was no evidence of them. The mixed rock-strewn and boulder landscape appeared to me undomesticated, untouched even by human imagination. I do not say this with certainty. I state this with plain and unmodified ignorance. We walked away from the pass with desperation, and that does not seem to me now, as I write this, abnormal. Everything I have ever read about people going to passes, it appears that they go through them with some desperation.

As we walked down I began to see the isolated patches of gentians, so minute in the vast landscape that they seemed like colorful pebbles. And so too were the little croppings of *Delphinium,* six inches high at most, pale and hairy hoods of whitish, grayish blooms. They were in bloom and we were in the month of October. Where could we find seeds? But this is a plant so particular, it needs a certain amount of time covered with snow and then a certain altitude on top of that. It was another wonder to see, and it made me think of the great Alpine gardener who lives not too far away from me, Geoffrey Charlesworth, but I only thought of him, I do not know him. It also made me think of once going to a part of Glacier National Park, with my friend Ian Frazier, and walking in an Alpine meadow and seeing the plants that will grow on rocky soil, exposed to the harsh elements of sun and wind, thrive with abandon. The walk down was treacherous, each step seemed a passport to doom, a mix of rocks and boulders, as usual, but in this part of the world, the usual was always new. And then I noticed, there, something new: the rocks and boulders had darkened; the very openness of the sky had taken on a darker tinge, as if another dominance reigned.

We stopped for lunch in a sheltered part of the valley and the sun was hot, and there was no wind at all, and just as we were congratulating ourselves on how well everything was going a host of black clouds appeared on the horizon and they did not go away. They came toward us and we packed up and walked on. They hovered, not so much overhead but in the background, like some evil omen to come. We then walked along the edge of a landslide; that is to say, what might have been an easy path to walk on had fallen down, and for a short while I understood what was meant by a knife's edge in the context of people walking on mountains. We walked to Topke Gola and again were in acres and acres of rhododendrons, all low growing, shrubby, and small leaved; and juniper, *Salix,* and of course *Meconopsis* (we were seeing it in abundance, the full-of-seed capsules of *paniculata*), and *Arisaema jacquemontii* (a plant in seed I found, but Dan had to tell me its exact identification). We walked through such a vast area filled with masses of small-leaved rhododendron that I was sure for a short time that there was no such place as Topke Gola. In this vast area covered with the small-leaved rhododendrons, there were some remains of camping sites, of campfires, and sleeping or outdoor habitation. And I then understood the herds of yaks that I had made way for coming over the pass. I was in the middle of a vast pasture. Everything that was a treasure to us in our gardens in Wales or North America was fodder in the life of yaks and the people who took care of and depended on them for sustenance. We walked through this wide and high valley, the mountains in the near distance (for by now everything far away was nearby and everything nearby was far away) and exhausted as if for the first time, without remembering that we had been exhausted before, and after a while we saw the hamlet of Topke Gola way in the distant. After the two nights spent in the forest, seeing a village with houses, and so therefore people and domesticity, seemed like a gift. And like a gift it held within it surprise, perhaps the essential, wonder, beauty, and mystery. I could see its brown structures, unsullied by paint of any kind, that were the dwelling places, huddled together, as if each one was a part of the other. From above and at thirteen thousand feet, the whole hamlet seemed so nearby, always so nearby, but it took one and a half hours from first seeing it to arriving there, and buildings that from far away seemed so small and insignificant were large and stairs had to be climbed to enter them. Not ever did I get used to this—the deceptive nearness of my destinations—not ever did I become accustomed to the vast difference between my expectation, my perception, and reality; the way things really are.

When I arrived at our campsite everything was all set up. We were a little village all by ourselves. Sunam, Thile, and Mingma seemed happy, I supposed it was because they had gotten us to Topke Gola safely. Their happiness made me love them, whatever that means now and especially then. It was decided we would spend two full days there. It was an area rich in flora to be grown in various temporal zones, certainly for people who made gardens and were prosperous enough to

Village of Topke Gola

afford the plants that would be grown from the seeds collected here. The porters had built fires from twigs gathered from the junipers and rhododendrons, which were growing everywhere. It was as if they regarded the junipers and rhododendrons as weeds. But I am reminded again that every weed can be made into a treasure in the right circumstances. The junipers and rhododendrons being burnt for fuel then would be a treasure to many a gardener in the climate I am living in now, it would be a treasure in North America.

Seeing my pitched tent then, it was as if I was seeing my ancestral home, and I laid out my sleeping bag in it and crawled in. We were at three thousand feet lower than we had been at the pass and the whole day just passed not like a whole day at all but like many days, each part of the day so different, as if it were something in a View-Master, that child's toy-way (at least it was a child's toy when I was a child) of viewing scenes, every detail in one photograph, every detail contributing to a full realization of the picture, every picture being such a realization of what was real, that the real was always lacking. And so Topke Gola, seen from far away, was like a picture, but then when arriving in it, it had its problems: some people were living there and they did not come out to greet us, and the buildings that when seen from above had been so mysterious and full of promise, now nothing emerged from them. It was as if we had stumbled onto something that had been and yet at the same time was in the present. The hamlet was closed and yet the hamlet was completely accessible. I experienced it so.

We had a dinner of rice and dahl and potatoes and I had been noticing that over the last five days the potatoes had become impossible to eat. I had thought that Cook just grew tired of cooking potatoes and didn't care whether they were worth eating or whether they were cooked properly or not, but Sunam explained to me that the potatoes were cooked in a pressure cooker and that the higher we got, the high altitude nullified the power of the pressure cooker to cook food thoroughly. It was just as well, for I went to bed, that is, I crawled into my sleeping bag, just as it got dark at half past seven. In truth, it felt like midnight. I left Dan and Bleddyn and Sue, cataloging and labeling and cleaning the collections made so far. Perhaps I was suffering from the altitude, but I felt nothing so much as tired, physically, of course, but also mentally for I needed one year, it seemed to me, to absorb all that I had seen that day alone.

Let me recount: I began on the bank of the blue glacial stream with Sunam's special breakfast, I crossed it, walked up a valley filled with rocks and boulders that were the conductors of rivulets sometimes, streams sometimes, and then we were at the foot of the pass and we walked up that for two hours, making way for herds of yaks that were on their way to Tibet, and we saw a lake, discreetly placed away from the human eye, and then we walked down a ravine and into a rocky meadow, a grazing pasture for yaks, past masses of plants, each of them a treasure to grow in my garden if only they would allow themselves to do so, and then I walked into a hamlet, a fabled place, and I rested there. I went to bed and the next morning woke up to the ritual of all the other mornings: a basin of hot water brought to me by the assistant to Cook, a cup of hot instant coffee. I drank the hot beverage; I gave myself a sponge bath and got dressed and walked out of the tent I shared with Dan to breakfast. It took me a while to realize that my tent was cast on, that I had slept on, and that I was also walking on, an area in which *Meconopsis* (in particular *paniculata*) grew wildly.

After breakfast I did some housecleaning in our tent. The day was beautifully clear, the sun shining, the skies blue and cloudless. And yet there was a chill in the air that did not correspond to the bright sun and the clear sky. It was as if all three things existed apart from each other, one not an influence on the other. The sun could shine as brightly as it wished, in as cloudless a sky as there ever could be, and the air would remain a temperature that was not affected by any of that. I put out Dan's and my sleeping bags, laying them out on some small-leaved rhododendrons and the juniper and berberis that grew everywhere. I put out also my dirty and worn-up clothes, hoping that exposure to the sunlight and the clean air would make them smell and feel better. I asked Cook to warm some water for me so that I could take a bath. He did and brought me the aluminum washbasin in which all our dishes were washed. He filled it up with water, hot and cold to make just the right temperature for a bath, and I washed myself using a bar of soap that I had taken from the expensive hotel when I had stayed overnight in Hong Kong on my way to Nepal, such a lifetime ago, or so it seemed. That was the bar of soap that we used to wash our hands before each meal, part of the ritual of being served our meals at a table that was always formally set with a tablecloth and knife and fork in their proper place. The soap had come in a blue box with the Tiffany label and the further away we got from anything resembling the idea of Tiffany and the luxury it represents, so did the soap become grimy and slimy from falling into dirt and being closed up in its expensive little soap box. Cleansed with the help of the by-now disgusting Tiffany soap, I put on my aired-out dirty clothes and felt wonderful.

Topke Gola, I could now see, was not a village or a hamlet, it was a place. Chyamtang had been a village, Thudam was a trading post, a crossroads connecting one place with the next. Topke Gola was a holy place. There was a monastery there and perhaps a Holy Man was in it. Sunam never said yes or no. He said, though, that in the summer many people lived there, that all the buildings are occupied then, but after that most people leave and only a few of them stay behind. He bought some yak meat from someone who had stayed behind and that night we had it for dinner, the first fresh meat we had eaten since we left Kathmandu. We were at a little under twelve thousand feet in altitude, four thousand feet below the altitude at the pass. Like all the other days before, what had taken place yesterday seemed like a dream. Topke Gola seemed like a dream too. Or perhaps another way of putting it, I felt as if I was looking at things through a sieve, not a transparency, but a surface with small holes in it. I could see the monastery, a small whitewashed building in a sea of brown. How did the whitewash get all the way up here? I wondered, but that was all I could do, for I got the impression that I shouldn't go anywhere near it.

In Topke Gola, there was a sacred lake, a mile above the village, a destination for pilgrims who came to the village in the summer. I walked up to it. As usual in this place, I was in awe at the unexpected. How could I predict that there would be a body of water, a lake, not at all like the secret one seen from above the pass, that finds its way to the River Ganges? That lake, the one seen from above the pass, was so remote and it seemed as if it would remain so even if you found yourself sailing on it. It was as if, because it would become part of a body of water that was accessible to so many, it made itself available for viewing purposes to only a few. The Sacred Lake in Topke Gola on the other hand looked sacredly domesticated. A goddess is said to live there and in the temple, a beautiful little open-sided building situated at the entrance to the lake, were the remains of offerings, bone, branches, stones, and a small bottle of whiskey. On its banks were growing many things I desired as a gardener: rhododendrons, juniper, berberis, clematis, and so on. I turned away from this and walked back to our camp, exhausted, not from going to the Sacred Lake but from knowing that it exists. And why is that? Why not have that feeling from seeing the lake above the pass, that lake being a true secret? If someone doesn't point it out to you, it will be missed altogether. I believe it is because seeing something that is hidden in the natural world makes me think not at all about myself, not about any one thing in particular; that a body of water situated in an area of the world with which I am not at all geographically familiar fills me with the joy of spectacle,

Handwoven prayer rug in Topke Gola

the happiness that comes from the privilege of looking at something solely rare and solely uncomplicated. But the Sacred Lake plunged me into thinking of the unknowableness of other people.

Later that day, Sunam took me to a weaver, a woman who lived all year in Topke Gola and made prayer rugs by a handloom. I bought one and only after I got home to Vermont did I see that it was somewhat crooked, it had not been evenly woven.

Those two days and three nights spent in Topke Gola were perfect. The nights were cool and it rained then. The days were sunny, with the clouds dark and heavy with moisture or white fluffs of clouds without moisture, flitting hurriedly to some other destination. Sue and I stayed in camp and cleaned seeds, glad for the days of rest; Dan and Bleddyn went off to the mountains above and came back with treasures of seeds. The porters made fires from the wood of the treasured rhododendrons and junipers and berberis. They sang songs and made and ate their food along with us. I realized then, that I had no idea how or when they acquired or ate their food. They sat around with Sue and me and she taught them how to separate various seeds from their fleshy fruit. They knew nothing. Those three nights and two complete days seemed, even then, but more so now, as if they were the sole purpose of our journey. Everything collected there was growable in a Vermont garden. I was keenly aware of that. When coming down into Topke Gola that very first day, I had spied an *Arisaema* in seed and Dan had made a big show of it for he had been looking for it. And all the *Meconopsis* in our area were ones I could grow, if only I would learn to do so. Where I live, this is not the sort of plant you can just throw its seeds on the ground and wait to see what happens. We were surrounded by thousand-foot-high, green-covered mountainsides and above these were snowtopped peaks. Coming out of one side of the green-covered mountain was a fierce waterfall that looked, in its usual way, as if it had been painted on there, so constant was the force of its flow. But unlike the other waterfalls of this kind, the long white foam falling silently into an invisible abyss, this one was so close by its constant roar was unrelenting. Sometimes, due I suppose to some distortion caused by the wind or some other natural element, it sounded like the roar of jet engines. But if I had never heard the sound of jet engines, I do not know what I would liken it to. Those two days were like that, perfect and perfect again, unerring. When we had soup made of yak blood and then a stew of yak meat all in the same meal, it was perfect. When during the night and the next day, our stomachs ached in upset at this sudden change in our diet, which had been high in carbohydrates, it was perfect. No error at all, no complaints. What nights we saw: no full moon lighting up the star-filled sky now, just a part moon, the biggest spot of light in a deep navy blue sky, seeming motionless, wherever it appeared, just the way the earth we're standing on seems motionless. I marveled again and again at how every time I stepped out of the tent Dan and I shared, I was walking on a carpet of *Meconopsis paniculata*. And then we left.

Our leave-taking perhaps began with our arrival. That first morning after we had arrived the night before, Jhaba Lama said goodbye to us and returned to his home in Chyamtang. He had agreed to be with us only as far as Topke Gola and at that juncture of our journey, Sunam had calculated that we would need less help. As things unfolded, he was correct. Sue and Bleddyn and Dan and I said goodbye to him and gave him a tip, a generous one, and we gave him that large of a tip because we thought he would take it home to his parents and make their lives a little easier, especially we were thinking of his mother. Immediately on receiving this large sum of money he bought a drum from another porter and began playing it with the biggest grin on his face, a grin that I took to express his own satisfaction at getting something he really wanted. All along the way, while we had been going to bed early and fretting through the night in one form of sleep or the other, the porters would stay up and drink and sing and dance to music they made. Someone had a drum, a small one that had to be held between the knees, and Jhaba Lama had liked the sound of it and he liked to dance to the sound of it. And so he bought the drum with his own money. He left us and would spend the night in Thudam and then reach his village, Chyamtang, the next day. He would make our four-day journey in two days.

We left Topke Gola, the place that had ten houses (I had counted them), and a sacred lake with a good amount of seeds, from which would come plants for gardens, at half past seven in the morning. It was cold, thirty-three degrees Fahrenheit, and some new snow had fallen on the mountain up above us. But we were not going up, we from now on would be going down. I did look around me one last time, not so much to say goodbye, for I feel, even now, that I shall go to that place again; I looked around for a last look with the thought that it would not be too long before I doubted that I had ever been in such a place.

A NIGHT SPENT IN A GORGE

We left Topke Gola on a Saturday but I had no idea what that meant. When I am at home in Vermont, on a Saturday I do things that I do not do any other day of the week. When leaving Topke Gola on that day I had nothing to remind me that it was Saturday. We set off the way we had done all the other days when setting off. How strange it was to exist with a purpose, with something to do, something to be engaged in, but to have no sense of a time in which to place it. We had a routine all right, we were awakened by someone bringing us a cup of a hot beverage. We then were each given a bowl of hot water to clean ourselves and we did so. We

got dressed, we ate our breakfast, which often was a delicious bowl of oatmeal and honey and hot milk. We filled
our water bottles, we packed up our day bag, and we set
off. We stopped for lunch somewhere, rested a little bit,
and then we set off. At around half past three, usually we
were starting to settle down for the night. It got dark,
we ate dinner, and at around eight o'clock we were in
our sleeping bags, in our tents reading, or chatting and
then going to sleep. That was pretty much our day and
our night. That was our routine. And yet there was
nothing about it that was taken for granted. The day
was always new, the night was always new. Except for
the stops in Chyamtang and Topke Gola, we spent
each day and each night in a different place. Our routine was constant movement and constant change; our
routine was the new. But the new is not a routine. It
was unsettling, feelings were sometimes hurt, tempers
sometimes got lost. For the days we walked before
coming to Chyamtang, Bleddyn complained about the
route, especially after he had to pass up a trip up to the
Barun Valley. Dan and I complained that our bags were
never in camp when we got there and we had to stand
around in our wet clothes and wait for the porters. Once
the porters had gotten drunk and gotten into camp way
after the day had turned into night. Sue never complained. I whined constantly, particularly about the

bathroom situation. There was none. Each place we camped, a small tent was put up over a hole that that been freshly dug in the ground. That was our toilet. After we left camp, the hole was filled with dirt and it was made to look as if nothing had taken place there. I almost never visited the small tent with the hole in the middle of it, and I whined about it but mainly to myself.

That day we left Topke Gola, a Saturday, was exactly like all our other leave-takings and yet we were leaving a place unlike any other place we had been to before. I am now remembering how quiet it was, yet how full of sounds it was, but the quiet was only the absence of sounds I had been used to and the sounds were ones I had never heard before. The water falling out of the mountain, down into an abyss I would never see again, for instance. And its falling down seemed eternal, unchangeable, whether I could see and hear it or not. Three nights and two complete days in Topke Gola felt like a year. The actual span of a year, 365 days, spent in a place like that would be an eternity for someone like me. Within a year, you can remember the beginning and from that anticipate the future and the end. It was with Topke Gola in mind and all that had come before that I walked forward. Crossing over a bridge (made from the trunk of some wonderful gardenworthy tree, that was growing nearby) with a loud rage of water beneath us, we crept away, with nothing to make us sure we had really been there but our memories, and the rug and yak bells we had bought and the many collections of seeds that had been collected. That loud rage of water was the Mewa Khola and we traveled along its banks without paying attention until we met its confluence, joining up with an even larger body of water, the Tamur River, but that would be many days later. At this moment, I could almost certainly be convinced that I had not been to such a place as Topke Gola or slept on a carpet of *Meconopsis* and everything else besides.

We walked down now, going up also, but mostly we were going down. As when, at the beginning of our adventure, attaining any height meant we had to also go down, so now too, going down meant also going up. We walked through yet again another beautifully forested area of oaks and maples but the farther down we got, each hundred yards or so, brought me to things that would not thrive in my garden in Vermont. Not the *Panax*, not the *Strobilanthes*, not the *Cremanthodium*, not the *Sarcococca*, some of which was fragrantly in bloom, some of which had already set seed. We walked for a long time, too long, and dropped too rapidly, and eventually, when we stopped for lunch at half past two, the seed collectors were angry. That valley we had just descended warranted at least a day of exploring. We started out that morning at twelve thousand feet or so and by lunchtime, at half past two, we were at eight thousand feet. In that part of the world, the difference between temperate and tropical is altitude, and in losing altitude we were losing that thing called the hardy plant, the plant that will live through winter, that time when the gardener is driven indoors.

Oh, the sadness of it. For there wasn't one truly flat place for hours. It was as if, once we were going down, we could only do so, just go down. The morning was beautiful, clear, cold at the start and then the lower we got, it became hot and then hotter in that insufferable way of the days before Topke Gola. Suddenly we came upon a clearing, an open area, and there was a little building, a cattle shed. By then, I knew where there were cattle, I couldn't grow the plants growing there. To whom did it belong? It wasn't occupied right then but we could see a pile of ashes, where someone had built a fire recently. That was where we stopped and had lunch, almost seven hours after we left Topke Gola that morning. If I had been told that it was seven days later instead of seven hours, I would not have been surprised. A big debate ensued: should we camp at the spot where we were having lunch and from there we could explore the valley back up to just below Topke Gola? Should we retreat, going back over the way we had just been? The valley we were descending into was rich in plants that could be grown in a zone such as the one in which I live, but also plants that were more tender than that. The botanists, Dan and Bleddyn, decided that we should make camp at the place we were having lunch, and so they told Sunam that is what we would do. But Sunam told them that the porters carrying our luggage, and the tents, and other essential things were miles ahead and could not be reached. Dan and Bleddyn insisted that someone race ahead and tell them to return. It is possible Sunam did this, it is possible he didn't. How could we know? We didn't understand Nepali. In any case, Sunam told us that the porters had refused to come back. They had descended quite a bit, thousands of feet. They would not come back up carrying all those loads of stuff. This was understandable. The path we were on was steep, rocky, and the rocks were wet—not moist—wet. In any case, I think they were tired of us all and our walk and rests for lunch or some other kind of break, and then our resuming the walk again and rest for the night, and our demands that they devote themselves to our needs, such as arriving in camp before us and setting up camp so that we could arrive to something we regarded as home. The sudden rebellion by the porters shocked us. They had been so nice to us, so kind; now, we wondered if all along what we had thought were encouraging words, spoken to us in their native language, was really them mocking us, finding us and our obsession of their native plants ridiculous, worthy of jokes made just before they fell asleep. But we had paid for this and we demanded that they return and make our camp where we wished. They didn't come back up, and a bitter, sour mood settled over us. We ate a delicious meal of tinned fish and vegetables and then started to walk again.

At around four o'clock in the afternoon as we started to descend into the bottom of the valley the sun disappeared, leaving behind a light that seemed to come from a long distance away, a light struggling to reach us. It started to rain, at first just a steady drizzle; by that time we had gotten used to the rapid change in the weather and thought, hoped, that perhaps it was just a phase, the rain would fall and then suddenly stop and then suddenly turn into sunshine. But the rain did not stop, The drizzle grew and grew into a full shower. Sue and I were walking alone, Bleddyn and Dan were behind us, the porters and Sherpas were ahead of us, looking for a flat place for us to spend the night. Sue and I stopped and took shelter under a massive outcropping of rock that had been arranged in such a way that it looked like a natural domestic dwelling place. Many people must have taken shelter there, for in a corner was a makeshift fireplace for cooking and keeping warm with ample space left over for sleeping or just taking shelter, the way we were doing. The rain did not let up; in fact it came down harder than I have ever experienced rain falling anywhere before. And I thought this: if weather ever becomes an economic commodity, this part of the world would dominate the market for it. Every way in which the weather can manifest itself represents the ideal way for it to do so. The hot sun was the best hot sun I had experienced. The cold nights defined such a thing as the cold night. The snow on the pass going over to Topke Gola seemed a snow that other snow might imitate. The domed sky seemed to be the place from which skies were made and then dispatched to other parts of the globe. The water falling down from this sky was rain but it had a different consistency, it wasn't pelting and it wasn't torrential, it wasn't gentle and it wasn't soft, it just came down and coated everything it fell on with its supersaturated moistness, making every-thing slippery and unstable. We had to walk carefully now, for any misstep might lead to a broken bone, and that would be a disaster for the person with the broken bone. We walked down and down into a seemingly bot-tomless gorge until, just before the light of day vanished forever, we came to a place where the porters had made our camp.

How they divined such an area, I will never know, for it was not a normal place to make a camp, it was hell. We were at the entrance to a deep gorge and above us towered its granite sides, moist with water seeping out of every tiny crack of its surface. A beautiful magenta-colored *Impatiens* grew on the sides of this wall and so too did some kind of small-leaved *Rhododendron*. We were in the midst of a thickly growing patch of *Edgeworthia,* a plant that I had only seen in illustrations before, my interest in it limited to that because I can't grow it in Vermont. It was beautiful, as all those things are when seen growing in their natural habitat, growing without restraint, growing not to be observed or appreciated or possessed by any gardener. Where our tents had been set up, a large patch of *Edgeworthia* had been cut down and thrown aside to make way for us. What a pity, just the way it was a pity when Dan saw the *Viburnum* that is a treasure in his garden near Seattle all bundled up as fodder for a domesticated animal way back in the village of Chichila.

We had supper of mostly potatoes and they were cooked more properly than the last few days, all because we were at a lower altitude, but I didn't have much of an appetite. I crawled into our tent and my sleeping bag. It rained and rained all through the night and I prayed that nothing above me would become dislodged and crash down on me. Nothing did. That next morning we practically ran out of there. Everyone, the plant hunters and the people supporting them, just left in the greatest hurry. We walked out of the gorge, carefully threading over the rocky, muddy, slippery path. It was dark and cold all the way through until three hours after we left we came up into the thick sunshine of a beautiful day. At the top, we rested and tried to be jovial about the night at the bottom of the gorge. Soon, like all the rest of our experiences, it seemed like a figment of our imagination, for so pleasing and dramatic was the scene in front of us. A wide vista of green forested mountains reaching up to touch that everlasting blue cloudless sky and the mountains themselves reaching down into a valley, the bottom of which we could not see. The day before, at lunchtime, I had seen a boy who was not of our party, passing us by shepherding some cows, heading in the same direction we were. Now I saw him again but he was going toward the place I had seen him the day before, the place where we had lunch, the place I might never see again. And it was brought home to me again, that while every moment I was experiencing had an exquisite uniqueness and made me feel that everything was unforgettable, I was also in the middle of someone else's daily routine, someone captured by the ordinariness of his everyday life.

We stopped and ate lunch in a hamlet just before Donje, the place where we would camp for that night. It was so pleasant, so magical really. It seemed to be a minor monastery, lots of prayer flags covered the outside area of a place for doing holy things, like praying. The extended family living there was very friendly and did not show us any sign that they found our sudden presence among them mystifying. Sunam bought some fresh vegetables for lunch, something we had not had for a while, and when we noticed that the wife of the house had a foot-manipulated weaving machine from which she made the beautiful aprons that the women in that part of the region wore, we wondered if we could buy some. She had none freshly made so the one that she was then wearing was sold to us. This craven behavior on our part can be explained: we were becoming afraid that there was less and less evidence to show, to ourselves only, that we had done what we thought we had done, that we had been to the places we had been, and the impressive collection of seeds that we had made seemed not enough. From there we could see our night's resting place, the village of Donje. We could see its yellow painted buildings; we had not seen painted buildings for a while.

We got to Donje at about half past two in the afternoon. The sun was still out in full, making it hot and dry. There was not a cloud in the sky. But this village was a place that I most probably had read about in a newspaper in my part of the world under the heading of "Dateline" or something like that. Maoist guerrillas had driven out the Nepalese authority at gunpoint. A building that had housed the police was burned out, empty inside, just its walls still standing, a ruin. The school building was intact, but it was shuttered up and the familiar red letters were written on its outside. Above the village itself stood a beautiful white building, a temple, and it stood out from the other buildings because of its siting and color, pristine white, while the other buildings were painted a creamy yellow. That building was shuttered up because the Maoists forbade religion. The school too was shuttered up, but Sunam said it was in observation of a holiday. I wanted to know what holiday it was, but by then I had come to see that every time we were in a village, starting with just after Num, and there was some unexpected difficulty, Sunam would say a holiday was being observed. I didn't doubt him at all.

No sooner had we set up camp than the Maoists appeared. At this point, setting up camp involved taking out all the seeds that had been collected, five hundred packets so far, and laying them out in the sun to dry. Some of them needed further cleaning, more washing, more separating from the chaff. Perhaps that moment is one of many that holds in it a metaphor of the very idea of the garden itself: we had in our possession seeds that, if properly germinated, would produce some of the most beautiful and desirable flowering plants to appear in a garden situated in the temperate zone; at the very same time we were in danger of being killed and our dream of the garden in the temperate zone, the place in which we lived, would die with us also. At the very moment we were projecting ourselves into an ideal idyll we were in between life and death. The Maoists appeared in a way we had never seen them before, belligerent, loud, and serious about the Maoist business. A few of them looked like people from Tibet but most of them looked like people from India. They wore badges of the red star on the lapels of their jackets or shirts. They wanted all of us to sit down and listen to them but succeeded in only Sunam and Thile and Mingma and some of the other Nepalese doing so. We—Dan, Bleddyn, Sue, and I—couldn't understand anything they said, for they were speaking in Nepali, and so kept drifting off to take care of the seeds. Cook had to take care of dinner. Sunam, perhaps knowing of what we would encounter later, had bought three chickens at the place where we had lunch and Cook was busy murdering them and cleaning them and making them into a meal. The Maoist lecture lasted all through the afternoon into the setting sun. They mentioned over

and over again the indignity of being called mere terrorists by President Powell of the United States, and then
they left. Their departure did not lessen the tension in our
camp. Sunam, trying to make us less tense I suppose,
went off and found us some chang. It was forbidden in
Maoist-controlled areas, so acquiring it was very secre-
tive and yet drinking it was so elaborate. For it it had
to be drunk from large wooden containers, the size of
jugs, made from bamboo, through a straw made from
bamboo also. It tasted terrible but I must have drunk
enough of it because I got drunk. After staggering back
to our tent, and lying in my sleeping bag, I could hear
the rest of them—Dan, Bleddyn, Sue, and the rest of our
party—for a long time afterward. Later than that, I
heard great loud booming sounds and thought they
were landslides; but Sunam told us that the sounds we
heard were the Maoists perfecting their bombs. In the
middle of the night, when I staggered out of my tent to
go take a pee, I was afraid I would be killed by the
Maoists, but I could also see that the night sky was clear
and full of stars and perfectly innocent of whom I might
wish to harm and who might wish to harm me.

We walked away from the experience of spending the
night with seeds of flowers we loved while all the time
vulnerable to people who might not like us and decide
to do something about it. We walked through a village

that was one of their headquarters, down to the Mewa Khola, and crossed it happily under the illusion that we were free of them. I saw a begonia, something that looked like a houseplant growing on the side of the Mewa Khola. That shocked me. We passed a little building, a house of worship in the middle of this thickly forested area on this river's banks. We walked, knowing the area of real seedworthy collectibles was behind us. We had lunch in an unexpected grand place. We came upon a lone dwelling, prosperous with animals, pigs, and cows, an abundance of areas carefully cultivated in which were growing grains and vegetables. The dwelling place itself was carefully painted: newly painted-on whitewash, and brown diamond-shaped stencil patterns ornamenting the area just beneath the roof. We were on the banks of the Mewa Khola and we could hear it roaring toward its final destination. Sunam pointed out to us the path he had originally wanted us to take. To say it was a mile above is not an exaggeration. We had to crane our heads back quite a ways to see the path he had thought for us to walk. We then walked on that afternoon through areas that had become forested with poinsettia and *Datura,* plants that are native to Mexico. They were in bloom, both of them with trunks as thick as maple trees in Vermont. We crossed roaring streams that made a false step positively dangerous. We descended mostly, crossing fields of millet and then finally landed in the village, Phapung, that had a banner with the red star running across it. It had in it four little shops, each of them selling the same things, and for some reason that made it seem safe. How to explain it? Four little shops, each of them filled with exactly the same amount of dirt and disorder or dirt and order, the same little bars of soap for sale that are a staple in motels in North America. All the men wore the same little hats, the shape of a carefully molded sharp-sided pudding, on their heads. Some of them seemed pleased to see us (and that made us suspicious), some of them seemed angry at us (and that made us uneasy), some of them seemed indifferent to us (and that made us suspicious), in other words, we were not feeling comfortable being there.

We walked down a bank littered with feces, human and animal, to the river and washed ourselves, knowing full well that it brought with it whatever the people above us had deposited in it. But we were desperate to renew ourselves and water always offers the illusion of that, renewal. And so we walked through the stench and tried to clean ourselves. We were not clean and we felt it. We ate a supper of noodles, the exact concoction that my son, Harold, likes to eat all the time, ramen noodles, only it was made by some company in India, not Japan, the way his is. Strangely, this Maoist-controlled village was not at all frightening. Beer and cigarettes were forbidden here, and perhaps that was what reassured us. All the passions were under control. Right then, calm strangers were a blessing to me.

In the morning, after the usual rituals, we set off and by that time our journey, which was at its end, began to resemble its beginning. We walked and walked, only this time going down, and we passed by many people going toward where we had just come and many more than that passed us going toward where we were heading. We saw the same, unidentifiable to me, birds flitting by and heard the same screeching sound of a mill grinding grain. We could feel we were getting closer to the end of the adventure. Suddenly the path was teeming with people, most of them looking more like people who come from India than like people who come from Tibet. Our presence, mine especially, drew less stares, less curiosity. It was in the middle of the day, when we were exhausted finally from the walk and the heat of the sun, and upset at the amount of rubbish everywhere, that we looked and saw there was a half-dressed Englishman making his way toward us and carrying an umbrella. He was as astonished to see us as we to see him. He had heard of Dan and Sue and Bleddyn, though they had never heard of him. He was making his way up the valley, through the very paths we had just come down, and looking for the seeds of plants also. He was going up to Topke Gola and then over to Thudam, for he was interested in finding the seeds of rhododendrons. Months later, Dan told me that this man had met some Maoists in Thudam and that they had robbed him of everything, even his clothes, and treated him badly altogether, and that he was lucky not to have been killed by them. But at the time we saw him, we were filled with envy that he was going back to where we had been and perhaps would find things that we had missed, especially on that awful day when we made the rapid descent from Topke Gola to the night spent in the gorge among the *Edgeworthia*.

We spent the afternoon walking on cliffs high above the Mewa Khola, which by then was a furious mass of water, crossing it as it joined up with the Tamur River. We meant to spend the night in the school yard of the village of Handrung but the entire school of children, none them seeming more than twelve years old, boys and girls, poured out of their classroom and surrounded us as if we were living examples in a number of school subjects combined. They came closer and closer, until we could see spending the night among them would be a nightmare. Sunam then took us across the Tamur, above where it met the Mewa Khola, and we made a camp on its banks. On the way to that campsite, we found a restaurant and store and they sold beer, and we bought many bottles and sat in the river naked and drank it. With the exception of that frightening night when the Maoists came and Sunam, to calm us, found us some chang, we had not tasted alcohol since leaving Num. Sitting on the banks of the Tamur, a river so sure of itself, it did not need to rage to look dangerous, just flowing along, with an abundance of little wavelets peaking here and there, but the wide span of it made me take it seriously. We all clung to its sandy banks, no one making bold gestures to swim into the powerful moving flow.

And here is something I shall never forget. I left my fellow travelers and went off to find a place to pee. I went off some ways, alone, away from the porters and the Sherpas, somewhere I thought it would be impossible for me to be seen. I was wearing only my hiking bra and underpants and so I felt exposed enough. In what I thought was a private moment, I proceeded to pee. Before I squatted down, I saw a mass of deep blue and light blue, but it was so far away on the opposite bank of the river, I couldn't make anything of it. And so while squatting and peeing, I decided, just out of my own curiosity, to wave to that mass of deep and light blue.

When I did so, it not only waved back to me, it let up a cheer. I continued to pee and they continued to stand there looking at me.

We drank on through the evening, staying up later than we had ever done since we left Kathmandu. I stood outside and saw bats, the size of pigeons, swooping around me, hunting for insects that I could not see. That night was clear and bright, as usual, and if my dense brain had ever been able to understand the arrangement of the bright lights in the sky, I would have had even more enjoyment. I went to bed. We were drunk but I more so than the others, and the next day, walking up to Taplejung, the town that formally signified the end of adventure, as Tumlingtar had signified its beginning, I had a hangover that made me feel I was dying. At no other time in this period of walking in altitudes that must have surprised not just my body but my very being itself, did I feel so demoralized and ill.

IT IS FINISHED

I had been told over and over again that to get to
Taplejung, we would descend to the Tamur River,
which was just under three thousand feet, and then walk
up to Taplejung, which was at about six thousand feet.
That morning when we started out for Taplejung, I
found it hard to believe that the walk would be as difficult as it was described. I had covered a few thousand
feet in a day on this trip and by now was used to long,
tedious ascents. Of course, I had not done it with a
hangover. We started out in that village above the
Tamur River, a village beautifully kept, with many terraced gardens, full of vegetables, squash, beans, corn,

and ornamentals, mostly plants, such as marigold and *Datura* and poinsettia. Along the way, from time to time, we would find a place for resting, a bench placed beneath a canopy of the *Ficus* love trees.

I walked up to Taplejung, passing through beautifully carved-out terraces, on which were growing food that I, a person who grew up on an island not far from the Equator, was familiar with. All around me was that lush growth of the tropical zone: corn, a plant native to the southern region of the Americas; potatoes, originating from that area also and hard-shell beans; and then nothing that I recognized for eating, just woodland, and the *Ficus* trees decorating the roadside at a place where it was comfortable to stop. There were many well-dressed people, men in suits for instance and women in dressy dresses, all wearing flip-flops and all walking with more confidence and speed than we, in our expensive hiking boots. Along the way the clouds hid Kanchenjunga, which was just an arm's-reach away, or so the distance made you think and feel. We looked and looked, hoping for that predictable unpredictableness, the weather changing when it seemed that it would never do so. But the clouds remained in front of Kanchenjunga, keeping it out of our view; and the sun shone on above us, pelting us with its rays without any letup. I struggled on, feeling sick, really sick for the first time, lagging behind everyone, with nothing to console me, certainly not the thought of some wonderful thing to be found that would be a supreme pleasure in my garden in Vermont. We passed by an army outpost, and that was frightening, for everything associated with the government was a potential target of the Maoists. We finally got to Taplejung and it made me sad to think of civilization. It was a crowded maze and a mess. Every fruit I knew of, apple, orange, pineapple, could be found as juice pressed into a bottle there. Every animal I knew, pig, cattle, chicken, its flesh free of bones, could be found in a tin there; fish too, there were tins of salmon and tuna and mackerel.

I bought a tin of corned beef and asked Cook to prepare it for lunch. Sunam somehow arranged for Cook to make us lunch in a restaurant. The view, right up to the cloud-shielded Kanchenjunga, was incredibly beautiful. While we waited for lunch we sat on a lawn, and on benches at that. The lawn was to be the place where our tents would be cast and we would spend the night. But the idea of spending the night in a city, hot and noisy with people going on with their lives, made us unhappy. It was hard to imagine that just a few nights ago, we were resting with the quiet and isolation of Topke Gola, that when I stepped out of my tent, I walked on stands of *Meconopsis* and *Primula* and tried to avoid, as I walked

Author packing up for the trip home

about, getting entangled in *Berberis* and juniper and small-leaved rhododendrons. Even the sky now was open in an ordinary way, no longer domed, suggesting the reality of the earth's shape and that we were magically, tenuously, hanging on to its surface.

Dan then had a talk with Sunam and they began to make plans for us to walk to the airport, to Suketar, a place where there was no residing, just the place from which planes came and went. We were told it was five miles above us, but at the time, it seemed five hundred miles. Perhaps it was the end of the journey, perhaps knowing at reaching Suketar, there would be no garden, by which I mean no fruit-bearing plants that would yield seeds for me to collect and imagine comfortably flowering in the garden I have made in Vermont. Bleddyn found some *Codonopsis* in fruit and a few seeds on the way there, but they did not seem to be specimens new to us, we had encountered them earlier, and we all walked on with indifference. Suddenly, leaving our surroundings became paramount, just as at the beginning, leaving Kathmandu, arriving at Tumlingtar and all that it entailed, was paramount. So too leaving at the end had about it a desperation and cravenness. We wanted to leave and our destination was beyond Kathmandu, our destination was home and the comfort and beauty of our gardens. On the way up to Suketar, we saw many people walking down from that direction. They paid no mind to us, we were not worthy of attention in any way, we were not new to them. The airport at Suketar is a trailhead for Kanchenjunga. We reached the airport and found it filled with Nepalese soldiers armed in the usual way of soldiers and that the airport had a tightly enforced curfew. All lights had to be out at exactly eight o'clock and they would shoot with the intention to kill, without question, at anything to be seen moving after that.

A gloominess set in. We were at a trailhead for Kanchenjunga. There are a few ways to get to Kanchenjunga and where we were was one of them. A group of Italians who had just returned from base camp there was camped nearby. There was also a group of Germans. As Americans and British people, we felt free to make fun of the Italians but in a kind way. As Americans and British people we not only made fun of the Germans, we also hated them. For one thing, they had the best spot for camping at the airport. Places like the airport were common targets for the Maoists to attack, and the Germans, because they got to the airport before we did, had camped in a relatively protected area away from the potential line of fire. When we got there, the only place left to camp was the most vulnerable spot to be in: directly between the army and the Maoists. We had a dinner of noodles from a package with its accompanying flavorings at a restaurant that was owned by a beautiful woman who looked Tibetan and who told us that her husband was an officer in the Royal Nepalese Army. Dan and I couldn't quite decide whether that, her husband being on the government's side, was a good thing or not from the point of view of our eating in her restaurant. What if Maoists hated her in particular because of her husband's work? The next two nights we ate at other establishments. Certainly by eight o'clock each night we were all in our tents in our sleeping bags and the entire area became dark and quiet. We heard nothing from one side (the Maoists) or the other (the people defending the airport from the Maoists) and were so glad when the morning came without event.

By that time I became sick, really so, feeling unable to get out of our tent, could not even eat breakfast or any other meal, only drank water and went to the little tent that had been set up as an outhouse for us to expel matter that I had not even expected I had in me. For three days I lay in my tent waiting for an airplane to come and pick us up. Those days were bright and hot but the landscape in the distance, which held Kanchenjunga on one side, Makalu on one side, and Everest in the distance beyond that, remained veiled; and regarding all of it, I felt as if I was in the middle of a fable, a live one. For without doubt, those magnificent and legendary landmarks of the Himalayan landscape were all there but they were mostly hidden from me all the time I lay within sight of them. One day, through the mist and much cloud, Sunam pointed out some white piffle far away and said it was Makalu, and then I couldn't remember if he said it was Kanchenjunga. Now, I do not care, for Dan and I have decided that we would like to walk around the baseline of that mountain and so, even then, in the middle of not knowing if we would survive our time at the airport and the tension between the Maoists and the people defending the airport, we were thinking of ways to get back here, ways to look at the landscape and find plants that would grow in our gardens.

Those days at the airport, lying inside the tent in my sleeping bag naked, because I felt so sick that I thought I was dying, and dying then felt like a reasonable alternative. It wasn't the unexpected last-minute decision to walk up from the airport that did me in. It wasn't the hangover from drinking the equivalent of a bottle and a half of beer the night before when we were resting on the banks of the Tamur River that made me feel my own death was nearby. Certainly not being afraid of the Maoists starting an attack on the airport where we camped just as we were camping there. It seemed to me that I wilted from the cumulative effort of walking over and passing through the Himalayan terrain. The experience of having the day ahead of me teeming with an unfamiliarity that was a dramatic departure from any unfamiliarity I had been used to; the experience of having the day just passed seeming like something I had dreamt and yet its reality clung to me: I had collected some seeds within this dream, and as I was lying inside the tent all day sick, Dan and Bleddyn and Sue were cleaning and drying and labeling and numbering the bounty outside. The days were clear, the sky without clouds, the sun beaming down, and yet it was chilly. In the distance, in one direction lay Kanchenjunga; in the distance in the other direction, looking west, lay Makalu; but even the distance itself was all hidden in a shroud of clouds.

By the end of the third day of staying at the airport and hoping that the Maoists would not attack it, we were able to leave. We said goodbye to the porters and everybody else who had been with us since the beginning. Dan lamented that there had been no proper farewell of dancing and feasts and tears like the time eight years ago when that seed-collecting expedition had come to an end. But better no ceremonial goodbye and safe departure than a ceremonial goodbye followed by disaster. We got on an airplane, the kind that is always pictured in fatal accidents involving people from rich countries in the process of experiencing the world as spectacle. Everything went well. Through the windows of the plane, I saw the whole range of high peaks that are in Nepal. They looked like something on a calendar, permanent and in place day after day, month after month, year after year, a backdrop against which time passing is marked off. Days later, in Kathmandu, we heard that the very airport where we had camped for days, waiting for a plane to come and get us, had been attacked by Maoists and some people had been killed.

We spent three days on the roof of our hotel in Kathmandu, cleaning and drying seeds, labeling them, numbering the packets, getting them ready to be inspected and shipped out, after proper inspection by the proper authorities, to our gardens in Wales (for Bleddyn and Sue), Kingston, Washington (for Dan), and North Bennington, Vermont (for me). The weather was blessedly perfect for this: hot and dry, cloudless skies. As at the beginning, I saw the laundry of the same family hung out to dry on a clothesline on top of their roof. An orange tree, loaded with green fruit three weeks ago, was now equally loaded with ripe fruit and from time to time someone would come along and shake the tree, hoping to get the ripened fruit to fall down. The Himalayan crow, a bird of solid black feathers interrupted by a band of gray, like a necklace around its neck, flew overhead in its familiar unsettling way. When night came, we gathered up the packets of seeds, admired the fruit bats, which filled the night sky in almost the same way the crows had filled the day sky. We ate breakfast, we ate lunch, we ate dinner, all in a restaurant.

Dan, Sue, Bleddyn, and I were sitting on the roof among the seeds that had been gathered when suddenly we heard a loud noise, an explosion. It did not sound like thunder, it sounded like a bomb. We looked out and saw a black tunnel of smoke coming from a building nearby, perhaps one quarter of a mile away. While looking we heard and saw at the same time a loud noise and an impenetrable, black, ball-shaped cloud coming from a structure not far from the first one. We heard a third explosion but could not see where that came from. The Maoists had called a strike. All transportation was to come to a halt. All places of commerce must be closed. We gathered up our seeds and put them away until the next day, when they were shipped out after being inspected and the proper people allowed us to do so. And then we waited to leave this place, Kathmandu, Nepal, which held in it the dreams I have of my own garden. I remembered the carpet of gentians, seen as I was ascending up to the pass on the way to Topke Gola and on the descent from that. And then the isolated but thick patches of a *Delphinium,* six inches high, grayish, bluish, and hairy, abloom in the melting snow. There were the forests of rhododendrons, specimens thirty feet high and with their barks peeling off, an added interest. I never knew rhododendrons, seen packed up against a house, could have an added interest apart from the one packed up against a house. I remembered all that I had seen but especially I remembered all that I had felt. I remembered my fears. I remembered how practically every step I had taken was fraught with the memory of my past, the immediate one of my son, Harold, all alone in Vermont, and my love for him and my fear of losing him. I love the garden, my love for it had brought me to this place, walking in the foothills of the highest mountains on the earth looking for flowering plants, which were not endemic to my part of the gardening world, but would thrive in my garden. As I remembered the beauty of the deep blue starlit sky at night, the days of sunlight brightness and distorted distances, the days of walking among forests of maples and oaks and rhododendrons and bamboo, always at that time I was thinking of my own garden.

As I walked and observed, each plant, be it tree, shrub, or herbaceous perennial, seemed perfect in its setting or in its sighting. I was in fact looking at Nature, or the thing called so, and I was also looking at a garden. The garden is an invention, the garden is an awareness, a self-consciousness, an artifice. We think and feel that we are making something natural when we make a garden, something that, if come upon unexpectedly, is a pleasure to behold; something that banishes the idea of order and hard work and disappointments and sadness, even as the garden is sometimes made up of nothing but all that.

Eden is never far from the gardener's mind. It is The Garden to which we all refer, whether we know it or not. And it is forever out of reach. As I walked up and down the terrain in the foothills of the Himalaya looking for plants appropriate for growing in the garden I am now (even now, for the garden is ongoing, and a stop to it means death) making in Vermont, the strangeness of my situation was not lost to me. Vermont, all by itself should be Eden and gardenworthy enough. But apparently, I do not find it so. I seem to believe that I will find my idyll more a true ideal, only if I can populate it with plants from another side of the world.

ACKNOWLEDGMENTS

I would like to thank Jeffrey Posternak especially, especially. And also, Philip Fisher and Elaine Scarry. And also Annie Shawn and Harold Shawn. And also Uncle Sandy and Aunt Annie. And also Wayne Winterrowd and Joe Eck. And also Sunam and Thile and Mingma. And also William Bartram, Joseph Hooker, Frank Smythe, Roy Lancaster, Daniel J. Hinkley and Sue and Bleddyn Wynn-Jones. And also Larry Porges, whose kindness and skill will not be forgotten.

ACKNOWLEDGMENTS